WAY
of
ZEN

Tenshin Fletcher
& David Scott

Thomas Dunne Books
St. Martin's Press ♒ New York

THOMAS DUNNE BOOKS
An Imprint of St. Martin's Press

Way of Zen
Copyright © 2001 by Tenshin Fletcher & David Scott

For information, address:

St. Martin's Press,
175 Fifth Avenue,
New York,
N.Y. 10010.

ISBN 0 312 20620 8

First U.S. Edition: June 2001

10 9 8 7 6 5 4 3 2 1

The publishers would like to thank the following for the use of their pictures:
The Art Archive: p. 12, p. 14, p. 17, p. 21, p. 26, p. 61, p. 73, p. 154. Camera Press:
p. 29, p. 33, p. 36, p. 50, p. 69, p. 78, p. 85, p. 87, p. 112, p. 114, p. 121, p. 129,
p. 130, p. 133, p. 145, p. 168. Hulton Getty: p. 49, p. 82, p. 160, p. 171, p. 174.
JNTO: p. 141, p. 142. Stephanie Merzel: p. 186. David Scott: p. 53, p. 136, p. 151.
The illustrations on pp. 106–107 are by Alan Roberts.

Contents

Acknowledgments

To the lineage of awakened Zen Buddhist teachers embodied in my own benevolent teacher, Hakuyu Maezumi Roshi. Without his teaching this book would not have been possible.

In the trenches I would like to acknowledge David Scott, my co-author who had the initial inspiration and did all the work of stringing this together. To Mary Yugen Courtney for reading, correcting, inspiring, and clarifying, and to all those who helped write it all down: Jason Buhle, Arthur Wayu Kennedy, Jeremy Jokan Stuart, and Philip Shinko Squire.

To Ann Seisen Saunders Sensei, for her many efforts in all directions to get this book in gear and to my mother and father, Bill and Barbara, for acting as the "man in the street" and being there.

Finally, for those trying to transmit the Buddha's teaching in the West. You have my sympathy and deepest appreciation.

Tenshin Fletcher

Zen Mountain Center

P.O. Box 43, Mountain Center, CA 92561

Tel: (909) 659-5272 Fax: (909) 659-3275

E-mail: zmc@zmc.org

Web site: www.zmc.org

Genpo Merzel Roshi, Abbot of the Zen Center, Utah. Roshi's teaching, patience, kindness, and wisdom are the bedrock on which my practice is founded and is sustained. Tenshin Fletcher, Sensei, teacher and friend, for his indomitable spirit and complete dedication to the work of the Dharma. Despite his busy teaching schedule, it has been a spacious experience, a delight, and a privilege to work with him. I have learned much in the process. Tony Doubleday, Harry Cook, and Richard Smith, three good friends, for their great help and research work in the writing of particular sections of this book. Janet Wheeler for her editorial work and welcome suggestions. Helen Robinson for her invaluable last minute proofreading. Finally, thank you to Helen Kokelaar, a wizard on the word processor and, as a bonus, also a very nice person to work with.

David Scott

Author's Note

The intention of *Way of Zen* is to provide an introduction and a practical insight to the history and development of Zen; to the Buddhist tradition on which it is founded; to the practice in daily life on which it depends; to the cultural arts that it has inspired; and to its contemporary situation and future in the West.

Way of Zen will be of worth to any reader interested in the broad exoteric dimensions of Zen, while for those who wish to get deeper into its heart the book also provides information and insights into the day-to-day reality of Zen training and advice on how to proceed in the practice.

This combined exoteric/esoteric approach, based on the dual experiences of the authors—one grounded in long traditional monastic training, the other in lay practice—gives this book its particular flavor. We trust that it will recommend itself to new and seasoned practitioners and to the general reader who wishes to explore deeper than the surface of this apparently enigmatic, but in reality very direct tradition.

In writing about Zen Buddhism there is the question of which translations to use for the names of Zen masters and Zen terminology. There are English translations of original Chinese names (using a variety of systems) and English translations of the Japanese translations of the Chinese originals, as well as straightforward English translations of Japanese names and terms. As you may imagine, it can become rather confusing to a non-academic. We have simplified matters by choosing the names and terms that are in most common usage, rather than imposing systematic confusion. On the first occasion that a person of historical importance is named, we give the date of birth and death where possible. Where this information is not given, the person concerned is (generally) either a contemporary Zen teacher or one who died recently.

We have used quotations throughout the book, but to keep it simple we have not always indicated its origins. The reading lists at the back of the book include all the books used in our research.

Tung-shan, a 9th-century Chinese Ch'an master, was a poet who was fond of teaching through the medium of poetry. One day, Tung-shan was crossing a stream and, seeing his own reflection in the water, was moved to write the following verse:

Do not seek the truth from others.
For thus it becomes further and further estranged.
Now that I go my way entirely alone
There is nowhere I cannot meet it.
Now it is just what I am,
And yet I am not it.
When this is understood,
Then one accords with Suchness.

Introduction

Japanese Zen, with its emphasis on the practice of za-zen, koan study, and the achievement of satori, has its origins in China, where the first Zen masters taught and the first recognizably Zen monasteries were founded.

However, the deepest roots of Zen are in India, where Siddhartha Gautama was born, attained enlightenment, and founded the Buddhist tradition. His life story is of more than historical interest since, for Zen followers, he is the model of one who has followed the Way to its end and achieved enlightenment. The Buddha (a Sanskrit word meaning "Awakened One") is no abstract figure of the past, but a man with whom a Zen practitioner might feel a personal relationship in his awareness of their shared struggles. Within the Zen tradition it is understood that each of us has the potential for complete awakening, and that the Buddha's path is not reserved for a special few but is definitely open to all.

This experience of awakening embodies the realization that Buddha-nature or essential nature, or suchness, is inherent in all people. Based on the pragmatic experience of many seekers over many centuries, Zen is above all a practical method of how to realize this experience and, in so doing, to see

This drawing symbolizes the Zen realization of Form is exactly Emptiness and Emptiness is exactly Form (circle, ink drawing by Zen Master Sengai, Japan, 18th century).

through to the essential nature of the universe and all things. For this reason, Zen has been called the "religion before religion."

We may substitute Tao, or God, or Ground of All Being, or another appropriate name for Buddha-nature; in this respect, the Zen tradition is a universal one. Anyone may practice it, independent of creed—indeed, the idea of being a "Zen Buddhist" may itself, like other concepts, be discarded.

A Zen characteristic, and one that separates it from other paths, is that it expresses the great matters of life and death, not in theological or metaphysical terms but in the here and now of everyday conversation and forms. Thus, when asked by a monk, "What is the meaning of Zen?" a Zen master replied, "Have you had your breakfast?" "Yes" said the monk. "Then wash your bowl," said the master. Another monk was asked the question, "We have to dress and eat every day, and how can we escape from that?" (That is to say, how do we go on living in the world, and at the same time find liberation?) The monk replied, "We dress, we eat." "I do not understand" came the reply. "If you do not understand, put on your clothes and eat your food," said the master.

Enigmatic answers that stop the intellect are a specialty of the Zen tradition. Zen masters are not interested in metaphysical concepts, but in answers unmediated by our notions and ideas. They want answers that manifest out of the experience of our own lives; those that are—in Zen parlance—"directly pointing at Reality."

A pragmatic outcome of having even a partial realization or experience of one's true Nature (or Buddha-nature) is that, for many, it leads to a much greater and more active acceptance of ordinary life, and paradoxically a recognition of its extraordinary quality. Everyday activities become invested with a delightful sense of wonder. Thus:

> *How miraculous, how wonderful!*
> *I draw water, I carry wood*
>
> Chinese Zen layman (Tang dynasty)

Zen's emphasis on the commonplace arises out of the understanding that, since unborn Buddha-mind is the true nature of our ordinary minds, then it must follow that Buddha-mind is to be found in the midst of our very own lives. Through za-zen and koan practice (which ask such questions as, "Who am I?" or "What is it?"), we become more and more familiar with ourselves. Paradoxically, out of this intimacy dawns the realization of our own emptiness and impermanence, which are no different from our Buddha-nature. In a famous passage, Eihei Dogen Zenji (1200–1253), the founder of Japanese Soto Zen, described the process thus: "To learn the way of the Buddha is to learn about oneself. To learn about oneself is to forget oneself. To forget oneself is to be enlightened by everything in the world. To be enlightened by everything is to let fall one's own body and mind." It is this falling off of one's body and mind that allows the entity commonly referred to as "oneself" to no longer be fixed. There is now only boundless, infinite, unobstructed space. However, it is most important not to become attached to this all-inclusive, unconditioned state of being. Zen emphasizes the need to move freely between the unconditioned and the conditioned. Hui Neng, the sixth Zen patriarch, had this to say about it:

The Infinite Ground is not for one second apart from the ordinary world of phenomena. If you look for it as such, you will find yourself cut off from the ordinary relative world, which is as much your reality as everything else. When you hear me speak of emptiness, don't become attached to it; especially don't become attached to any idea of it. Merely "sitting" still with your mind vacant, you fall into notional emptiness. The boundless emptiness of the sky embraces the "ten thousand things" of every shape and form—the sun, moon, and stars; mountains and rivers; bushes and trees; bad people and good; good teachings and bad; heavens and hells. All these are included in emptiness. The emptiness of your original nature is just like this. It too embraces everything. To this aspect the word "great" applies. All and everything is included in your own original nature.

The importance of not being attached to emptiness is graphically illustrated by the story of a Zen student who ran to his master, crying, "Master, master, it has finally come to me; all is nothing, all is emptiness. There is no me, no you, no thing." The master whacked him hard with a stick. The student wailed. The master exclaimed, "Tell me who was it, then, who felt the pain?"

The word Zen itself is an abbreviation of *Zenna* or *Zenno*, which is the way the Japanese would read the Chinese characters for *Ch'an-na*, which in its turn is Chinese for *Dhyana*. This is a Sanskrit word that describes both the act of meditation and the state of non-dualistic consciousness (or other states of consciousness beyond that of ordinary experience) that may arise from its practice.

As one would suspect from the origins of its name, the foundation of Zen practice is za-zen meditation, and its specific aim is to lead the practitioner to a full realization of his or her true nature. Zen teaches that the practice of za-zen is the steepest but quickest route to enlightenment, or "seeing things as they are." More than in any other school within the Buddhist tradition, Zen stresses the prime importance of enlightenment (you could here also use the word "realization") and ever-deepening enlightenment. In keeping with this, Zen requires us to drop all the various concepts onto which each of us hold in order to support the illusions that we imagine are necessary to sustain us. To this end, Zen masters make great use of contradiction and paradox. Less emphasis is placed on academic understanding, intellectual analysis, and ritual than in other schools, although this does not preclude their usefulness for some people.

Bodhidharma, Zen's first patriarch, succinctly defined those special characteristics of Zen that set it apart from other Buddhist traditions:

A special transmission outside the scriptures;
Without dependence on words or letters;
Directly pointing to the mind;
Seeing one's true nature and attaining Buddhahood.

Therefore, it is the case that the essence of Zen cannot be understood or experienced through the intellect, or expounded by academic argument. To get to its heart, one needs personal experiential knowledge. This is gained through training methods developed since the time of Bodhidharma, 1500 years ago. These methods may vary in detail, depending on the age, the culture, and the circumstance of their teaching, but the foundation of traditional Zen training is based on za-zen, koan practice (used mainly in the Rinzai school of Zen), *dokusan* (private interview with the teacher), and *samu* (a daily period of physical work, which brings the other training methods into accord with daily life). These specifically Zen essentials operate within the Buddhist fundamentals known as the Three Treasures: the Buddha, the Dharma (teachings of the Buddha), and the Sangha (a Buddhist community or grouping of people).

Be certain that this, or any other, book cannot give you a genuine experience of the essential nature of Zen, just as a cookbook cannot give you a taste of the dishes described. However, *The Way of Zen* provides a real insight into the traditions, values, and practices that underpin the Zen school, and a taste of the directness, compassion, humor, and absurdity that give Zen its unique and delightful flavor.

Pre-Buddhist India

The story of Zen starts at the time of the Buddha's birth. The teachings of the Buddha were influenced by contemporary beliefs, and were a reaction to the religious climate of the day. Understanding this background clarifies Buddhist beliefs, and, more specifically, the Zen Buddhist view.

The historical Buddha was born in India around 560 B.C. Indian philosophical thought at that time was largely influenced by the Vedas and the science of yoga, although, within these two schools, there were many different philosophical systems and religious movements. In the second millennium B.C., northwest India was invaded by a race of dynamic, patriarchal tribesmen who had migrated from the steppelands of central Asia. They spoke an early form of Sanskrit, and were part of what later became known as the Aryan race. The people they overran formed a sophisticated, matriarchal civilization that was now in decline. Out of this milieu evolved a culture that spread throughout India and ushered in the beginning of the Vedic Age (*c.* 1500–500 B.C.).

The Vedas are a vast, complex collection of scriptures that are divided into four sections. The oldest is the Rig Veda, a collection of over one thousand poems or hymns, some of which reflect on the origins of the universe, the nature of consciousness, and "Ultimate Reality." The Vedas are the oldest texts of Indian literature and are compositions to which orthodox Hindus ascribe divine authority. Their origins are not definitively understood, but it is widely accepted that the sometimes strikingly intuitive knowledge that they express was revealed to the seers and poets (known as *rishis*) during states of deep contemplation.

As the Vedas were initially transmitted orally from generation to generation, the Sanskrit language used in their telling became increasingly refined in order to lend expression to the mystical truths revealed to the rishis. Thus, in its final written form, Sanskrit, more than any language before or since, had a terminology that was able to classify and to describe stages of meditation and states of consciousness that lay beyond everyday experience, as well as the mental and spiritual processes that invoked them. Like Latin, Sanskrit is now a dead language. It remains the sacred language of Hinduism, since it was used to compose all of the religion's most important texts.

Indian king with Sadhus
(holy men).

The religious life of the Vedic Age was controlled by an hereditary priesthood called the Brahmin. Brahmin were at the apex of a social system structured by caste. Beneath them, in descending order of status, came the warrior and aristocratic classes; the merchants and other professionals; and the farmers. Later, a further grouping, probably formed from indigenous aboriginal peoples, became part of the system. They were known as Untouchables. They were deemed to have no caste. Despite this rigid caste system, which grips the country even today, India, at the time of the Buddha's birth, was a land of great spiritual energy, change, and religious liberalism.

The Brahmin believed (and still do) in an eternal, imperishable Absolute called—not surprisingly—*Brahman* (or Ultimate Reality, or the One-and-All-Pervading). Brahman cannot be explained or described linguistically. In religious texts the qualities of Brahman are referred to only in the negative, such as *Neti neti*, "Not this, not this." In its imminent human aspect, Brahman manifests as the *Atman*. Akin to the Western concept of a soul, the Atman is considered the real, immortal self of each being. Atman embodies absolute consciousness, absolute bliss, and eternal being. As a consequence, the classical Indian answer to the question of a man's true nature is "Tat tvam asi," "You are That."

In a revolutionary departure from this view, the Buddha, after his enlightenment, denied the existence of an Atman. His realization was that neither within nor outside any physical or mental manifestation is there anything that is of an independent, imperishable essence. In a discourse on Buddha Nature, Eihei Dogen illuminates this view in poetic but unequivocal terms:

The forming of mountains, rivers, and the earth is all dependent on the Buddha-nature. It being thus, seeing mountains and rivers is seeing the Buddha-nature. Seeing the Buddha-nature is seeing a donkey's jowls or a horse's mouth. The very impermanence of grass and tree, thicket and forest, is the Buddha-nature. The very impermanence of men and things, body and mind, is the Buddha-nature. Nations and lands, mountains and rivers are impermanent because they are the Buddha-nature. Supreme and complete enlightenment, because it is the Buddha-nature, is impermanent....

Our present moment-to-moment activity is the opening of a gate... Completely utilizing life, we cannot be held back by life. Completely utilizing death, we cannot be bothered by death. Do not cherish life. Do not blindly dread death. They are where the Buddha-nature is.

For infinite kalpas in the past, foolish people in great number have regarded man's spiritual consciousness as Buddha-nature, or as man's original state of suchness – how laughably absurd!... Buddha-nature is a fence, a wall, a tile, a pebble.

Buddhism did retain some similarities to Brahmanism, but the denial of the whole notion of Atman created a serious divide between the two teachings.

Even now, the negation of Atman leads some to assume that Buddhist enlightenment is attaining a sense of nothingness. On the contrary, as we shall see, the Zen experience is that the realization of one's true nature leads instead to a sense of spaciousness, freedom, and compassion.

Indian holy man in the yoga position.

Another contribution to the rich spiritual environment into which the Buddha was born, was an alternative religious outlook that had its origins in pre-Aryan culture. This was the yogic tradition, in which individuals or small groups would renounce the world and, in the solitude of caves, mountains, and forests, seek a direct knowledge of higher spiritual states without the intercession of a priesthood. *Yoga* is a Sanskrit word meaning "yoke," and in

Hinduism this carries the meaning of harnessing oneself to god. The yogi was seeking union with the Godhead. Theirs was a homeless, ascetic life that proved—to the aristocratic/warrior classes—more fascinating than the life of the Brahmin. Indeed, this was the path originally followed by the Buddha, later set aside for what he called the Middle Way.

Yogis variously practiced bodily castigations, shamanistic ceremonies, privations of food and sleep, the use of drugs and "magic" potions, and numerous other rites, as well as more conventional meditation techniques and study of the scriptures. Yogis were grouped by the Hindus according to the emphasis of their particular practice. For example, *Bhakti-yoga* practice stresses devotion to god, *jnana-yoga* is the path of knowledge, while *hatha-yoga*, the system best known in the West, is based on physical and breathing exercises. Their common denominator is the wish of each yogi to achieve union with Brahman and liberation of the individual spirit. Later, in the Mahayana Buddhist tradition of which Zen is a part, seeking for personal liberation was superseded by the bodhisathva ideal. The bodhisathva, out of compassion for all sentient beings, chooses to renounce entry into nirvana until all beings are saved.

This difference in aspiration arose out of the classical yoga view that each being is spiritually pure and free, but that in the course of being born becomes caught up or bound to the material or natural world. The yogi's task was to liberate his soul from this binding. Enlightenment led to a completely free, autonomous spirit, separate from the material world. The Zen Buddhist realization is that there is no division between the "soul" and the material world. The universe and everything in it is a seamless, interconnected, and thus interdependent, whole. From the Buddhist point of view, to realize this and to continue to strive for personal liberation would be as though your right hand chose of its own volition not to remove a painful splinter from your left hand. It is interesting the way these two views are exemplified in Zen and classical yoga meditation techniques. In Zen the meditator keeps his and her eyes half open, remaining part of the world while practicing interior calm. In yoga the meditator closes his eyes and focuses all his attention on inner contemplation; that is, he excludes the world.

By the time of the Buddha's birth, various yogic groups had begun to form, each rooted in the practice or philosophy of a particular teacher. Four main sects can be identified: the Skeptics believed the truth was unknowable; the Jains believed in the sacredness of all forms of life; the Materialists in the complete finality of death and thus the importance of enjoying life; and, finally, the followers of a teacher who taught that the universe was moving, albeit very slowly, toward ultimate perfection. A fifth sect, later to grow into the world-wide religion of Buddhism, was about to be founded.

The Buddha: His Life Story

The scene is set around 560 B.C., about 300 years after the Indo-Europeans had invaded northern India. The Shakya clan—Indo-Europeans residing in the foothills of the Himalayas—had a strange visitation. Queen Maya dreamed of being in a wonderful jeweled palace, where celestial maidens, caressed by falling flowers, bathed her. A majestic white elephant approached her, struck her on the right side, and entered into her womb. In the morning, she realized she was pregnant and told her husband King Suddhodana and the tribal elders. Sixty-four seers were sent for, and, after deliberating over auspicious omens, they agreed that the child was very special and would be either a great sage or a world ruler.

The Queen, who came from another province, wanted to have her baby at home where she would be more comfortable. On the way back to Devadaha, at Lumbini Grove in the neighborhood of Kapilavastu (now known as Padeira) in the north of the district of Gorakpur, she went into labor and a child was born. The circumstances, however, were quite unique. On emerging from the womb the child took three steps, pointed one hand to the sky, the other to the earth, and exclaimed, "I alone am the world-honored one." The child had a beautiful, golden hue and the thirty-two marks of an enlightened being. Unfortunately, Queen Maya died seven days after the birth from internal hemorrhaging. And thus was Siddhartha Gautama born. His caste was that of the warrior Brahmin and his title Prince of the Shakya clan.

One day, an old monk called Asita came by, saw the child, and burst into tears. The King asked, "Why are you crying?" "I am crying because I don't have long to live, and won't be around to hear your son's marvelous teaching. I only hope I can be reborn quickly so that I can study under him," the monk replied.

At this point, King Suddhodana decided to make sure that the prince did not become involved in religious matters, and began to organize the prince's life so that he would have no opportunity to encounter disturbing circumstances or religious life.

Young Siddhartha was educated in all the arts of his time. He excelled in the martial and courtly arts, he was taught science, philosophy, politics, and the ways of men, and he grew up healthy and strong.

Like the ruling class of the present day, he was well-guarded, doubly so because of the prophecies. When his servants became old or sick, they were removed. Before flowers died, they were removed. Everything was done so that sickness, old age, disease, and death could not disturb the boy.

Despite this, his own spiritual power could not be suppressed. At the age of twelve, he was at a country fair held in the palace precincts. His retainers wanted to dance and he did not. They were under strict orders never to leave him alone; nevertheless, he granted them permission and they departed. He sat there on his dais and began to focus on his breathing, experiencing such peace that he passed through the first level of meditation. On returning, his retainers were amazed by the self-absorption of the boy.

He led a peaceful life, and at the age of sixteen married his cousin Yasodhara, the daughter of the chief of Koli, and they had a son called Rahula. For a while, Prince Siddhartha was content with his life of worldly pleasures. When he was twenty-five, however, things changed. He began to feel the call of the world, craving more profound experience, and tiring of his life of luxury.

The anguish increased until, at the age of twenty-nine, he finally escaped the family compound and entered the bustling city. It was there that he first saw an old person, then someone sick, then a corpse—shock upon shock. Standing there, realizing that this was not just something that

Colossal stone statue of Buddha in niche at Bamiyan, Afghanistan (now destroyed).

happens to others, but would happen to him, he had the overwhelming desire to do something about it. At that moment he saw a home-leaver (a monk) and was impressed by the serenity on his face.

The impermanent nature of human existence struck him forcefully. He realized he could not follow his family duties.

'Twas not through hatred of his children sweet,
'Twas not through hatred of his lovely wife,
Thraller of hearts—not that he loved them less—
But Buddhahood more, that he renounced them all.

That night, Siddhartha left a note, escaped the compound, and crossed the Shakya borders into the province of the Mallas. In the town of Anomiya, he threw away his courtly clothes, shaved his head, and obtained the eight requisites of a home-leaver: three robes of patched, saffron-dyed cotton; a bowl for alms-gathering; a razor; a needle; a belt; and a water-strainer. He journeyed to Vaisali, the capital of the Urjis, and began to search for a teaching and a teacher. The teachings were varied at that time, ranging from self-immolation through praying for divine intervention, to mental discipline, good works, and ceremonial rites.

He settled down to study with Arada Kamala, who taught a method of one-pointed concentration and deep meditation. Having penetrated this teaching to the sphere of emptiness, he found Kamala had nothing more to teach. So he went to Rajagrha in Magaha and studied with Rudraka Ramaputra. Ramaputra's teaching conducted past the sphere of nothingness to the sphere of "neither perception nor non-perception." Siddhartha quickly mastered this rather difficult practice and Ramaputra proposed to set up Siddhartha as his teacher, but Siddhartha declined, as his mind was still not at peace.

He still had not solved his own question, "Why is there suffering, old age, disease, and death?" He went out into the wilderness, ate less and less, became more and more famous as an ascetic, and had over 400 followers. Still he was not satisfied. He continued his austerities until he was eating a grain of rice a day. Anyone who pressed his stomach could feel his backbone, all his ribs were clearly visible, his face was sunken, and his hair unkempt and matted. He was filthy and he had become a shadow of his former self. Still he continued. Then one day he was getting a drink of water from the river and fell in. Too weak to save himself, he would have drowned if a milkmaid, Sujata, hadn't pulled him from the river. Impressed by Siddhartha, she nursed him back to health.

He was ashamed that his efforts had nearly ended in his own death. All his austerities were for nothing in the light of Sujata's one compassionate act. He decided that he would sit until he resolved his question once and for all. In the meantime, all his disciples left him. Having seen him eating, they thought his practice had become degenerate.

At this point, Siddhartha realized that punishing the body for its own sake had not resolved his question. He had lived a life of empty luxury that had not worked. He had lived a life of renunciation that had not worked. So he started on a middle way, not falling into either extreme, directly dealing with the suffering, addressing the very question of life and death, bringing his mind to peace. He sat with unflinching resolve, losing track of time and place. Birds nested in his hair and spiders spun webs on his face and clothes, while deep within his being, all Siddhartha's energy worked to resolve this burning question.

Mara (the devil) came to test him, bringing all kinds of temptation. He promised riches beyond compare. He offered power: all the countries of the world bowing to Siddhartha. But he also threatened Siddhartha: if he did not cease his quest and bow to Mara, then his country would be destroyed and the Shakyas taken into bondage. Mara tried storms, fire, meteors, and dense blackness. Finally Mara brought out his gorgeous daughters, promising Siddhartha great pleasures if he would only stop. But Siddhartha had figured out Mara. He said, "I know your army. The first battalion is lust, the second discontent, the third is hunger and thirst, the fourth is craving, the fifth laziness and torpor, the sixth fear, the seventh doubt, and the eighth hypocrisy. Fame, gain, honor, ill-won glory, elevating oneself, and devaluing others. If this is your army, you cannot touch me." At this point, Mara disappeared and Siddhartha's mind cleared. He looked up and saw the morning sky. The morning star possessed his whole being, and he spontaneously exclaimed, "Wonder of wonders, I and all living beings simultaneously attain the way but because of upside-down views, we fail to realize it." His quest was at an end. "House of Ego, your ridgepole is broken and you will trouble me no more." Siddhartha Gautama, now Shakyamuni Buddha (the awakened one of the Shakya clan) sat in meditation, wondering what he could do with this realization. He was just about to give up, thinking it could not be taught to others: "I might as well enter into parinirvana" (i.e. die). Brahma, the king of the gods, came down and said, "Wait a minute. Of course you can teach it, somehow you will find a way." Shakyamuni, having let go of selfish desires, realized he had to live for others. Taking heart, he decided to try. He set out for Benares, the centuries-old religious center. He hadn't walked very far, when he met five of the ascetics who

*Monumental seated
Buddha from the 13th
century at Kamakura, Japan.*

had previously studied with him. They could see something in Shakya that they had never seen before and asked him to teach them.

His first teaching was the Four Noble Truths:
1. Life is suffering, being caught in our own illusions about life.
2. There is a cause of suffering. Suffering is based on our attachments to notions and things.
3. There is an end to suffering. We can see that all our attachment and desire is, in essence, empty.
4. The Eight-fold Path (the means to achieving the end of suffering), namely:
    1. Right thought or view.
    2. Right intention.
    3. Right speech.
    4. Right action.
    5. Right livelihood.
    6. Right effort.
    7. Right mindfulness.
    8. Right samadhi or concentration.

(We will discuss this, the core of Shakya's teaching in Chapter 4, Basic Buddhist Views.)

Hearing this, the five ascetics were deeply moved. They asked to be accepted as disciples, and were the first monks of his *sangha* (community).

The Buddha continued his journey, teaching in many of the northern Indian states. During this period, he converted Maudgalyayana and Shariputra, two of his chief disciples. Some of the Abhidharma, the philosophical part of the Tripitaka scriptures (see p. 32), are attributed to these two. Many of his great disciples, such as Mahakasyapa and Subhuti joined the Buddha during this period. Several kings were converted, including King Prasnajit of Kosala, King Udayana of Kausambi, and King Bimbisara of Maghada, who had invited Shakyamuni to instruct him before his enlightenment. He converted a bandit assassin, Angulimala, who was the terror of the kingdom of Kosala; Alauaka, the cannibal of Atavi; and Sunita, the scavenger, who was widely despised. These were difficult converts, but because of the Buddha's open personality and his facility with people, he was somehow able to reach them. As well as converting to the Buddha's teaching, two of his lay students donated the first monasteries (*viharas*): Anathapindika, the Jetavana vihara, and Visakha, the vihara at Purvarama.

These viharas were the first permanent sites where the community of monks and lay-people (the Sangha) could practice together. This type of training center has continued with strong, vital practice down to the present day.

Shakyamuni's greatest challenge, however, was returning to Shakya territory to teach. Just like Christ returning to his home town, he was perceived as the same old person. After initial difficulties, he managed to persuade them to listen by performing a miracle, spurting forth water and flame while walking in the sky. His wife, Yasodhara, was the first to be converted. Then his father, after seeing Shakyamuni begging, and trying in vain to get him to continue the royal lineage, heard Shakyamuni say, "My lineage is the most noble lineage of the Buddha's from beginning's time. How can I ever turn away from that?" Hearing these words, King Suddhodana resolved to practice the Way himself.

Shakyamini's half-brother, Nanda, converted on his coronation and wedding day, creating another unpleasant surprise for the Shakya clan who thus lost another crown prince. He was followed by Shakyamuni's son Rahula, another heir to the Shakya throne; Devadatta and Ananda, the Buddha's cousins; and Queen Prajnapati, his aunt and foster mother. These last three became important influences on the Buddha's life for different reasons.

Devadatta, after initially studying with the Buddha, became jealous of the Buddha's standing as a religious leader. With the aid of King Bimbisara's son Ajatasutra, he set up a vihara, hoping to become a great teacher. When his ambitions were not fulfilled, he made several attempts on the Buddha's life, but each one failed. Ajatasutra, feeling great remorse, abandoned his support of Devadatta and studied with Shakyamuni. Finally, Devadatta made one last attempt to 'see' the Buddha, but the earth would not permit it. He was swallowed up in an earthquake. Because of jealousy and fear, several attempts were made to discredit the Buddha, especially by leaders of other practices. Two accusations were directed at Shakyamuni by a former nun, Chincha, and by Sundari, a follower of a heretical sect, each claiming to have had sex with the Buddha. Both plots were exposed as false, but not without some damage. We are faced with the same human problems today.

Queen Prajnapati holds a unique place in the Buddha's life and in Buddhism, not only for being the one who raised the Buddha, but also for being the first nun. In those days, the position of women was extremely weak. The Buddha refused her ordination request three times, and she had to get Ananda to intercede on her behalf. Even then it took Ananda, the Buddha's most intimate companion, three attempts to get Prajnapati's petition accepted. The eight conditions she had to accept would be intolerable for women of today. Here are three of them:

1.   A monk, even if he has been ordained for only one day,
     is senior to a nun of a hundred years of practice.
2.   Nuns cannot rebuke or scold a monk on any pretext.
3.   Nuns may not reprove monks, but monks may
     reprove nuns.

Note: *These rules were observed in India, China, and Japan. A different appreciation of women's roles in the West is discussed in Chapter 10.*

To accept this, Prajnapati needed a great deal of humility, and a desire to practice that overrode all other concerns. Because of her efforts, women's practice in the Dharma remains highly inspirational.

Ananda was born at the time of the Buddha's enlightenment. He was so handsome that all the women fell in love with him. Even after becoming a monk and attending on the Buddha, he was often in trouble for chasing after women, or vice versa. The *sangha* (community) had to be very lenient with him and often found it difficult to accept him as a monk. Eventually, he did calm down and became a great champion of women, persuading the reticent Shakyamuni to allow women to be ordained. He attended the Buddha until the Buddha's death, and was his constant companion. Ananda had tremendous powers of recall, retaining all of the Buddha's words, and through supernatural powers he could memorize those talks at which he was not present. During the Buddha's life, he did not realize his true nature. When all the Bodhisattvas gathered at the Buddha's death to preserve his words, they wanted Ananda to attend. Only enlightened beings could attend, so he sat up all night in meditation, finally had some realization, and was admitted to the assembly. On hearing his version of the Buddha's words, they all agreed that what Ananda said was true. The Buddha's sutras all begin, "Thus I have heard." These are the words of Ananda. Eventually, this brilliant young man overcame his vanity and reliance on intellect to receive the Dharma as successor to Mahakasyapa.

With his simple teaching style, the Buddha gathered hundreds, if not thousands of disciples, always teaching at the level of the hearer's understanding. At the same time, he lived a life of a simple home-leaver: dressing in one robe, having one bowl, begging everyday for his own one meal, accepting with gratitude whatever was put in his bowl—no matter what! Sometimes he went hungry. Sometimes he would be given tainted food, sometimes delicacies, but he accepted it all to feed the body and allow the teaching to flow unhindered.

Each year he would do two three-month retreats, a rainy season retreat and a hot season retreat; during both times, the focus was meditation. These were times to enliven practice and put life into perspective. Then there were two seasons when the monks could relax a little and give the body some rest.

He taught like this for forty years, letting all come and study, never being alone, crossing caste boundaries, and encouraging all people to realize their nature.

At that point in history, there was no written record. So all of the Buddha's sayings were passed on orally. Many sutras (sayings of the Buddha) were passed on in this way until much later, when they were finally written down, usually in flowery language to aid recall. The variety of his teachings is remarkable, going through the whole spectrum of skillful meanings, from down-to-earth practical advice to profound esoteric imagery.

But most importantly, his living teaching continued, training people through example and through skillful means (*upaya*). Of his many enlightened disciples, the best example is Mahakasyapa, Shakyamuni Buddha's main heir. *Maha* means "great," and *kasyapa* means "light-drinker," because when Mahakasyapa was born the light was seen to be emanating from his mouth. He was already an accomplished teacher before Shakyamuni started teaching, and he already had over a thousand disciples. His asceticism was renowned throughout the land. His appearance was filthy; he dressed in rags, and was so emaciated that people didn't like to look at him. However, after he became the Buddha's student, Shakya would always seat him on his right-hand side (a place for a successor or equal) because the Buddha was so impressed with Mahakasyapa's insight and practice. After many years of intimate study, the Buddha held up a flower in front of the whole assembly, and out of hundreds, only Mahakasyapa smiled. Shakyamuni said: "You have the treasury of the true Dharmic eye, the marvelous mind of *nirvana* (peace), now I entrust it to you, Mahakasyapa." This was the start of the transmission of teachings, which has continued unbroken to this day. Approving of Mahakasyapa, seeing him hold true to his insight over the years, knowing that he would maintain it, he gave him the transmission.

In the kingdom of the Mallas at Kusinagara, after forty years of teaching, Shakyamuni Buddha went out on his daily begging round. Chunda, the blacksmith, offered him some *sukara-maddava*, which can be translated as either wild boar meat or pig food, a kind of bulbous vegetable. The Buddha realized that the food was spoiled, but ate it anyway so as not to offend the host. He warned the other monks to avoid that particular dish. The Buddha got sick and died. His last sermon, delivered from his deathbed, was on the four noble truths. After the Buddha's cremation, Ananda stood by the pyre in profound sadness. As a voice in his head, he heard the Buddha say, "I am the Tathagatha. As the Buddha Shakyamuni, I went from the land of the Shakyas and became enlightened at Bodhgaya. But, in reality, I have been enlightened from beginningless time, unlimited in the duration of life. I am."

What conclusions can be drawn from the Buddha's life? Certainly he was extraordinary, a larger-than-life character, yet in no way ego-centered. But in most ways he was like us, living the same existence, enjoying the pleasures of life, being puzzled about the nature of life and initially being distracted by money, sex, power, and fame. If there was one thing that made the Buddha stand out, it was his determination. Despite not knowing the outcome of his efforts, whether he would succeed in answering his question or not, he totally immersed himself until he was satisfied. Not stopping there, but struggling for expression, he found skillful means to enable all beings to experience the wonder of their own true nature.

The Buddha's encounter with Mara (the devil) has particular meaning for those practicing Buddhism. It is not simply that he met the devil and had all kinds of temptations. In a real sense he, you, and I experience this mara in the way we use our own minds. Remember that the Buddha, after six years, sat still in the midst of his troubled mind, no longer distracted by thoughts of what he could be doing, what he could attain, or by all kinds of entertaining fantasies (sex, fame, gain, and power). He decided to see reality as it is—stripped of illusion. If we can generate this resolve, then we, too, can overcome mara (all kinds of distraction). Then, like the Buddha, the wonder of life is revealed.

By "awakened", Buddha means awakened from our own ideas of how life should be. After Mara disappeared, his mind cleared, he saw distraction for what it is, he saw how his mind worked, and said, "Wonder of wonders, I and all beings simultaneously attain the way, but because of upside-down views we fail to see it." Seeing life as it is, he also saw the disease. The main problem for the practitioner is how he thinks, and how he takes that thinking to be the only reality. This means accepting that "I am not enlightened, therefore I need to think it out and go chasing after my vision of enlightenment," rather than studying the reality of our momentary existence, and illumining that. By experiencing our life directly, we begin to let go of reliance on thought. By not relying on thought, reality becomes unavoidable and clear.

In the Buddha's struggle to teach his experience, there is an important parallel with our practice. In Zen we say:

Manifest the ancient way
And express the inexpressible.

Reclining Buddha statue from Burma in gilded wood, early 18th century.

The ancient way is to practice—in the way we live our life. To express the inexpressible is to try to say something about our experience in live words, not dead explanation, that will communicate the reality of this realization to others. To attain a little enlightenment is one thing, but to express it is indeed difficult. In the attempt, our practice and realization is tempered and matured.

Thus Buddha taught for forty years, content to do the same things over and over. If you have tried this, you know this is no easy matter. Constancy is an important part of the practice. The Japanese word for practice is *narau*, to do the same thing over and over like a child. A child learning to ride a bicycle doesn't entertain failure. She just gets on, falls off, gets on, and falls off until, "Wow, I'm riding!" By just doing, we wear out old ways of delusive thinking until its weave becomes so thin we can see through it, and reality is apparent.

The Four Noble Truths, the Buddha's first teaching and his last, were the core of his teaching. Through experience this changed a little, the main difference being in the first three steps of the Eight-fold Path. These now became:

1.   Want little.
2.   Know how to be satisfied.
3.   Enjoy peace and tranquillity.

Having experienced human beings through forty years of practice, his teaching became simpler. Knowing the power of desire and how it is used is a critical aspect in practice.

If we want too many things, we cannot rest. Yet, if we have a few desires, there is a good chance that they can be satisfied. Satisfaction is on everyone's mind. First we find out what doesn't satisfy us, what causes us problems. It is our chasing after all kinds of things, never being at home in ourselves. "Now I have the Rolls Royce, I'm bored. I want something new, maybe a castle, then I'll be satisfied." We learn that chasing after things doesn't make us content. So we sit in the midst of those desires and use that energy to gain peace of mind. Soon, by channeling those desires and experiencing reality, we begin to enjoy peace and do not have to chase after all kinds of things. It's a very simple teaching that we can all apply.

The Buddha's teaching during those forty years was not contrived, but tailored to suit those involved. He forbade his disciples to use supernatural powers to convert people, as he realized that those people would then be practicing for those powers, not to liberate themselves and others. He exhorted his followers to see the truth for themselves, and not to think that Buddhahood just resided in Shakyamuni. "After all," he said, "I won't always be here." "Students, be a lamp unto yourselves, and being so, you can be a lamp unto others." The words in Ananda's head—"I have been enlightened from beginningless time, unlimited is the duration of life. I am."—are intrinsically the Buddha's life, the life that each one of us lives. It is always accessible right where we stand, but we have to do something to reveal it.

Unlike many religious leaders, Shakyamuni Buddha "walked the talk," practiced what he preached, and had profound experience to back it up. He never claimed to be more than a man—"awakened," but nevertheless a man. His teaching was no supernatural revelation, but one revealed through earnest endeavor and constant application. There is a line from an Indian *puja* (service) that states, "Buddha was a person as we are people. What the Buddha attained we too can attain."

The content of the Buddha's enlightenment is the basis of the survival of Buddhism. The Buddha experienced the unity of all things, and the self was forgotten. That dropping off of self-consciousness and self-concern gives us boundless freedom, and allows the natural stream of compassion to flow unhindered. Successive generations have experienced this for themselves, but that story is for later.

Buddhism in India

The Buddha died in about 480 B.C. The specific reason was food poisoning. It had caused him sickness and great pain, but he was said to have died with the same fortitude, patience, and concern for others with which he had lived. He was approximately eighty years of age when he died. For the times in which he lived, this was a long life. The Buddha died in Kusinagara, surrounded by followers, in a grove of sala trees. His last words of advice to the monks and lay people around him encapsulated his life's teachings: "All composite things are subject to decay. Strive diligently for liberation." Then he passed into Paranirvana, a state described in the sutras as dwelling in the experience of the Absolute:

As a flame blown out by the wind
Goes to rest and cannot be defined,
So the wise man freed from individuality
Goes to rest and cannot be defined.
Gone beyond all images—
Gone beyond the power of worlds.

Quoted in *Reflections on the Life of the Buddha*,
Garry Thomson, The Buddhist Society, London, 1983

A pilgrim prays at the site of the Lord Buddha's enlightenment, Bodh Gaya, India.

The Buddha's life was an auspicious event, since a fully enlightened being appears in the world only very rarely, and his death was said to have been mourned in every sphere of existence. Deities from all the realms crowded about his body so densely that a hair could not be slipped between them, while the sala trees, though it was not the right season, rained blossom over his corpse. It is natural in any age—but especially in the cultural milieu of the Buddha's time—that myth and folklore should surround the death of such a special human being. However, the very essence of his teaching is that he was not a god, and that his realization is open to each one of us.

Following his death, Buddhism spread throughout India. The very variety of Buddhist schools of thought that developed—later to spread far wider than India, to be absorbed into diverse cultures, including the

contemporary West—owes much to the Buddha's liberal humaneness. He foresaw that, with time, his teachings could lose their vitality. He wanted to leave matters flexible and not to create a rigid, codified system of beliefs or a religious structure. Above all, his desire was to help people see the truth and find their own liberation as an outcome. Thus, the following advice was given by the Buddha and recorded in the Paranirvana Sutra:

Be for yourselves your own flame and support. Let the truth be your flame and support, do not seek any other support. He who, from this moment, or after I have disappeared, is his own flame and his own support, will be a real disciple of mine, a disciple who knows how to conduct himself well.

The Buddha's encouragement of the spirit of free inquiry is further illustrated in the story of the Kalamas, a clan who lived in the city of Kesaputta in northern India. On a visit by the Buddha, an elder told him, "Certain holy men and Brahmin priests come to Kesaputta and teach. As for the teachings of others, they mock them. Then others come and do the same thing. As a result, whenever we listen to holy men and priests, we are full of doubt and waiver in uncertainty as to who is speaking truth, who falsehood." The Buddha replied, "Come, Kalamas, do not be satisfied with hearsay or with tradition or with legendary lore or with what has come down in your scriptures or with conjecture or with logical inference or with weighing evidence or with liking for a view after pondering it over, or with someone else's ability or with the thought, 'The monk is our teacher.' When you know in yourselves these ideas are unprofitable, liable to censure, condemned by the wise, being adopted and put into effect they lead to harm and suffering, then you should abandon them... [And conversely] When you know in yourselves these things are profitable... then you should practice them and abide in them."

From *Life of the Buddha*, Namamoli Kandy (B. P. S., 1978)

With this flexible, open outlook (described in Buddhist terminology as "skillful means") to inspire them, the Sangha of monks, founded by Shakyamuni Buddha, spread the Buddhist ideal by example and word. Initially, they were restricted to northern India, but later spread throughout the sub-continent. The advance of Buddhism as a popular religion, however, owed much to its patronage under Ashoka (274–236 B.C.), ruler of the Maurya Kingdom of northern India and an important figure in Buddhist history.

Ashoka was the grandson of Chandragupta Maurya, who by skillful military leadership and ruthlessness had forged an Indian empire. Ashoka, in the early years of his reign, also waged bloody campaigns to maintain his power. However, following a particularly cruel and destructive subjugation of the Kalinga (a people of east India, who had rebelled against him), Ashoka underwent a great psychological crisis of doubt. By chance he met with a Buddhist monk who, it seems, persuaded him of the benefits to himself and his people of using his authority to encourage peace and virtue as opposed to war and violence. Ashoka became a Buddhist, strenuously committed in the way that is perhaps the mark only of radical converts, and resolved to commence a "reign of Dharma."

Ashoka appointed special ministers to oversee the physical and ethical well-being of his people. Hospitals were built, monasteries founded, wells dug, vegetarianism propagated, and animal sacrifice forbidden. His stated ideals for a moral and happy life for his subjects embraced generosity, love of the truth, compassion, and inner insight. To this end, he had moral exhortations carved into rocks and pillars across his domain. For example:

Do not perform sacrifices or do anything else that
might hurt animals.
Be generous to your friends.
Do not get involved in quarrels and arguments.
Try to be pure of heart, humble, and faithful.
Do not think of your good points; remember
also your faults as well, and try to put them right.

Ashoka sent Buddhist missionaries to many other countries, apart from India, but had most success in Ceylon. Here, his son Mahinda laid the foundations for what would become a stronghold of Buddhist life, one maintained to this day. Ashoka also encouraged religious tolerance, and manifested it himself by giving patronage and freedom of expression to other religious communities within his empire. Ashoka's enlightened leadership, inspired by the teachings of Shakyamuni Buddha, popularized Buddhism among all the Indian classes. Before, it had principally been the domain of the more privileged in society.

Despite Ashoka's good works, the Maurya dynasty was eventually ousted, but Buddhism continued to thrive in India. Eighteen major schools of Buddhist thought are believed to have been established during the long course of Buddhism in India. However, by the time of Buddhism's decline at home and substantial dispersal away from Indian shores, two significant currents of tradition—the Theravadin and Mahayana—could be distinguished.

The Theravadin influence traveled south through Ceylon, Burma, and Thailand as far as Vietnam. The Mahayana school, of which Zen is a branch, moved north to China and finally to Tibet, where a distinctive Tibetan Buddhism developed. The story of the formation of the Mahayana school in India and its separation out of the early Buddhist Theravadin mainstream marks the early history of teachings that were later to become very influential in the formation of the Zen view, and thus the beginning of the Zen tradition.

During the Buddha's lifetime, and for 400–500 years after his death, his teachings were not recorded in written form. Their transmission was instead by word of mouth. Immediately after his death, to enhance the consistency of this transmission, a great council of monks and nuns gathered together from far and wide to establish a canon of law. Councils were also held for the same purposes at three later dates across a span of 400 years.

The first Council was convened in the city of Rajagriha, capital of the Kingdom of Magadha. It began at the beginning of the rainy season and lasted for seven months. Mahakashyapa initiated the Council. Traditionally, he is said to have questioned Ananda to establish the accurate context of the discourses of the Buddha, and questioned another disciple, Upali, about practical matters regulating the lives of the monks and nuns. There was further discourse with other elders to establish a consensus of opinion. Finally, the monastic rules (*Vinaya*) and Buddha's teachings (*Dharma*) were agreed upon, recited, and rehearsed. Thus equipped, the monks and nuns spread the teachings. There would obviously have remained differences of opinion and emphasis among them, and like-minded groupings would have formed, but the very nature of a verbal transmission reduced their divisive importance. Divisions could be overlooked without the precision of written text as a reference. In due course, however, the first complete written version of the teachings was eventually produced in Sri Lanka in about 80 B.C. The text was written in Pali, an ancient (now dead) Indian language, and was called the *Pali Canon*. This was a vast body of work divided into three main sections: the *Vinaya*, the *Sutra* and the *Abidharma* (hence its other name, the "Three Baskets"—*Tripitaka* in Pali).

The texts forming the Vinaya are chiefly practical instructions for the working of the Sangha, and rules for the behavior of monks and nuns. The sutras are texts that report the discourses of the Buddha. Each sutra, complete in itself, usually takes the form of a dialog in which a person comes to visit the Buddha and interrogates him on specific questions. The third division, the Abidharma, contains commentaries on the essential teachings of the sutras. Written in the form of metaphysical or scholastic texts, the expositions tend to

A Tibetan devotee puts a picture of the Dalai Lama to his head. Tibetan Buddhists, driven from their homeland by the Chinese invasion, have helped revive Buddhism in India, its country of origin.

proceed by the posing of analytical questions followed by enumerative responses. The Abidharma is the most recent of the three parts of the *Tripitaka*. Different schools have slightly differing versions. Later, Mahayana Abidharma texts were written in Sanskrit as opposed to Pali.

The Mahayana Buddhist School first arose as a reform movement at the time of the second great council (380 B.C.), but the *Pali Canon* texts became the axis around which differences of view within the Buddhist Sangha became properly defined. From then on, in a slow, organic fashion—as opposed to a radical split—the two overlapping traditions developed into separate schools.

The Theravadans invested more importance in the traditional teaching methods, ideas, and monastic rules set forth in the *Pali Canon*, while the

Mahayana branch of thought embraced a wider view of the practice. The special characteristics that evolved out of the Mahayana school, and those that separated it from the Theravadans, were its emphasis on the Bodhisattva ideal (see p. 89), and the new perspective it gave to lay practice and lay participation in the sangha. Those who expounded the Mahayana ideal offered it as a wide, accessible path, in which liberation was open to all, rather than the narrower, monastic tradition of the Theravadans, where liberation was viewed as the prerogative of monks and nuns. In the view of the Mahayanists, these were developments already latent in the Buddha's teachings and ripe for clarification and embodiment within the tradition. The Theravadan perspective was that Mahayana followers had moved far beyond the original teachings of the Buddha. In this they were probably correct, but the fresh thinking of the Mahayanists brought new vitality to Buddhism—an initiative one imagines the Buddha would have applauded.

To sum it up in simple terms, the Theravadan school believed in personal liberation (the Arhat ideal), the separation of Nirvana (spiritual liberation) from Samsara (the material world, our ordinary lives), and the prime importance of monastic discipline and rules of behavior. The Mahayanists were guided by the Bodhisattva ideal, by the view that Nirvana and Samsara are opposite sides of the one reality, and that involvement in a worldly life while remaining unattached to greed, anger, and ignorance is a valid way of life and possible path to liberation. One must add here, however, that within the two traditions, both historically and in the present day, there are, notwithstanding their different practices, profoundly realized men and women with the same deep store of compassion for all sentient beings. From the Zen perspective, one may safely say that a fully-realized Arhat is a Bodhisattva and vice versa. The separation of the two schools perhaps finally arose out of a dialectic controversy rather than deep fundamental differences.

There were many Mahayana influences on the later development of Zen thought, but two were of prime importance. The first, already mentioned, is the Mahayana replacement of the Theravadin spiritual ideal, the Arhat, with that of the Bodhisathva ideal. The second is the deepening of the teachings presented in the Prajnaparamita Hridaya Sutra by a man called Nagarjuna, and his related commentaries on *shunyata* (a Sanskrit word, for which "emptiness" is an approximate but inadequate translation).

Nagarjuna (A.D. 100–200), a great Buddhist thinker and, within the Zen tradition, considered the 14th patriarch of the Indian lineage, founded the Madhyamika or Middle Doctrine School. Nagarjuna sought to define the experience of Mahayana wisdom through his dialectic of Madhyamika. In the most simple of terms, his conclusion was that: "Things derive their being and nature by mutual dependence and are nothing in themselves."

Starting from the premise that each thing exists only in virtue of its opposite (e.g. hot/cold, weak/strong), he showed that all things are relative and without a basic essence—that is, empty. This emptiness, or shunyata, is the absence of an essence of things, but does not mean their non-existence as phenomena. Nagarjuna stated that it was false to say things exist or that they do not exist. The reality lies in the middle, in shunyata. It is the theme of Mahayana wisdom schools, including Zen, that it is only through *prajna* (intuitive wisdom) or shunyata (wisdom achieved through meditation) that one is carried to the other shore of liberation.

Shunyata, according to Nagarjuna, applies to all aspects of the phenomenal world, including the doctrines of Buddhist thought and practice, and even the notion of Shakayamuni Buddha and his enlightenment! However, shunyata as an absence of self-nature was a view that was in direct accordance with the teaching of the Buddha himself. The following is a short extract from the Tripitaka:

Ananda asked the Buddha: *"Lord, it is said that the world is suñña. But, Lord, in what respect is the world called suñña?"*

The Buddha answered: *"Ananda, as it is void of self or anything pertaining to self, so the world is called suñña."*

suñña = shunyata

For Nagarjuna, Nirvana and Samsara (the phenomenal world) are fundamentally identical. They are two forms of appearance of the same reality. In the *Maha Prajnaparamita Hridaya Sutra* (Great Wisdom Beyond Wisdom Heart Sutra), a basic Zen text chanted daily in Zen monasteries throughout the world, this is affirmed by the line: "Form is exactly emptiness, emptiness is exactly form." In his book *Heart Sutra*, Mu Soeng Sunim succinctly defines shunyata as follows: "Shunyata, then, carries and permeates all phenomena and makes their development possible. Shunyata is often equated with the absolute in Mahayana, since it is without duality and beyond empirical forms. In quantum physics, ultimate reality is equated with formless energy at the core of the atom. This energy (of physics) or shunyata (of Mahayana) is not a state of mere nothingness, but is the very source of all life and the essence of all forms."

The early direction and development of Buddhism in China also owed much to the Indian Mahayanist view. Kumarajiva (A.D. 344–413), China's most important translator of Sanskrit texts, was, in fact, an Indian Buddhist.

Kumarajiva entered a Buddhist monastic order at the age of seven. Later, he studied astronomy and mathematics, took a particular interest in the Mahayana Buddhist tradition, and went on to become a famous scholar. Kumarajiva was later captured by the Chinese and taken to China, where he was held captive for seventeen years by a general who was hostile to Buddhist thought. Finally, with the support of the Chinese emperor, he began the translation of Buddhist texts into Chinese. His works quickly became respected reference texts for scholars. With the aid of 800 other Buddhist monks, he created a translation center. Kumarajiva, unlike traditional translators of his time, was more concerned with conveying the essence of a teaching than in its word-for-word translation. Chinese scholars by the thousands flocked to him from all over the country.

A magnificent statue of Gautama Buddha, over 25 feet in height, in an ancient monastery of Ghoom, 4 miles from the great tea center of Darjeeling.

Kumarajiva supported and further clarified the Mahayanist doctrine of shunyata. He brought Mahayanist ideas into the mainstream of Chinese thought, and paved the way for the development of the Ch'an School, the precursor of the Japanese Zen tradition.

In India, by the 13th century, Buddhism had almost disappeared completely, remaining only in regions fringing the Himalayan foothills, and in Nepal. However, by then it had been established elsewhere. In his book, *The Long Search*, Ninian Smart romantically describes the dispersion of Buddhism from India across Asia to China and beyond as follows:

> It spread along the Ganges and westward to the Indian ocean. From the coasts it migrated to Ceylon, the first great Buddhist missionary endeavor beyond the landmass of India itself. Much later the sea routes could carry the faith to Burma and South-East Asia, down as far as Java, and even up to the coasts of China. But its most significant route was to the north-west, up into Afghanistan and beyond, where it came into contact with the rich cultures of Central Asia athwart the silk route into China and west to the Roman world. In the first century A.D., it had begun to percolate into China, and would thus be carried into those areas where Chinese civilization was influential: Vietnam to the south, Korea to the east, and across the sea to Japan.

Interestingly, in the last few decades in present-day India, Indians have begun once again to take an interest in Buddhism. Sacred sites are once more cared for and Buddhist monasteries are increasing in number.

In summary, the historical development of Buddhism in India can be approximately divided into four major phases:

1. The middle of the 6th to the middle of the 5th century B.C.:
    the phase of the establishment of the teaching of the Buddha and its transmission by monks and nuns.
2. The middle of the 4th century B.C. to the 1st century A.D.: the division and sub-division of the Sangha into eighteen major schools.
3. The 1st to the 7th century A.D.: the development of the Mahayana tradition.
4. From the 7th century: the emergence of Buddhist Tantra.
    By the 13th century, Buddhism was virtually extinct in India.

In conclusion, the life of Buddhism in India, from Shakyamuni's birth to its decline, is part of the Zen story and is fully acknowledged in the Zen lineage of patriarchs. In this lineage, those enlightened beings who ensured its generation-to-generation transmission are recognized and appreciated. The patriarchs listed are those great masters, each of whom received the Buddha Dharma from his master by heart-mind to heart-mind transmission. The lineage goes all the way back to Mahakashyapa, the first patriarch, who received his "transmission without words" from Shakyamuni Buddha himself. Afterward, Mahakashyapa made the same transmission to the disciple Ananda, who thus became the second Indian patriarch. The Indian lineage continues until Bodhidharma, who was the twenty-eighth in the series. Bodhidharma, who introduced Ch'an (Zen) into China, is at the same time the first Zen patriarch. The sixth Chinese Zen patriarch, Hui-neng, never transmitted the patriarchate formally to a successor and the lineage, in orthodox terms, ended with him. However, he had five senior disciples, from whom derive all the Dharmic successors of the various later schools of Zen. The outstanding masters of these lineages make up the remaining Chinese and Japanese patriarchs, recorded in the *Denkoroku*. This is a Zen text, composed by Keizan Jokin (1268–1325), which lists each of the patriarchs and records Master Keizan's accompanying teisho talks. In the *teisho* he gives a flavor of the great enlightenment of Shakyamuni Buddha and his nature, and the nature of those of each of the successive fifty-two patriarchs to whom it was transmitted. Out of veneration and appreciation for their great accomplishments, the names of the patriarchs are chanted as part of the daily service in traditional Zen monasteries.

Basic Buddhist Views

At the time of the Buddha, there was only the Buddha's teaching. After his death, the Theravadan Buddhist school came into being. From the Theravadan sect, the larger movement, the Mahayana, with a broad base of both lay and ordained followers, became influential. Out of this school came the Zen school. Mahayana means the great vehicle and the Mahayanists called the Theravadans the Hinayana, or small vehicle, as they felt that the Theravadan view was somewhat narrow. Although, in this book, out of common usage we sometimes refer to the Theravadan view as "Hinayana," no derogatory meaning is intended. It should also be realized that the bias of the views expressed here is toward the Mahayana, Zen. This arises out of the author's experience. In reading these views, it is important to realize that they are not beliefs to be taken as doctrine. They are expressions of reality for you to try out for yourself.

THE INTRINSIC VIEW

All Buddhist views come from the Buddha's enlightenment, and the path that leads to it. The content of the enlightenment is this: "I, all living beings simultaneously attain the way." This statement is sometimes translated as, "Wonder of wonders, I, all living beings, and the great earth have the wisdom and virtue of the awakened one." Over time we have forgotten this, yet on a deeper level we remember. It is that remembrance that causes practice to begin. Through practice, it becomes obvious that enlightenment has never been apart from us.

The Lotus Sutra illustrates this in the parable of the poor man and the jewel. One day, a rich man was walking down the street, when he saw a poor man. He was impressed with the poor man's demeanor and decided to give him some money. The rich man couldn't get the poor man to accept his offering, so, with the aid of a servant, he secretly sewed a valuable jewel in the poor man's coat and left the scene. A year later, he came back and, finding the man still poor, said, "Why are you still poor? Don't you know that you have a valuable jewel sewn into your coat?" The poor man was exceedingly happy when he realized this. Like the poor man, each one of us has this awakened nature, but we have to uncover it before we can use it.

EMPTINESS (Shunyata)

At the heart of the Buddha's realization is emptiness. This experience sets Buddhism apart from other religions, especially those having a theistic base, although it has been argued by certain Christian practitioners that this so-called emptiness is the face of God Himself. Language can only reach so far; terms like "emptiness" still cannot express the experience, but it comes closer than most words. There are other words used commonly to express emptiness, such as "the unborn," "uncreated," "true nature," "original self," and "the unknown."

The most famous of the Buddhist sutras is probably the *Maha Prajna Paramita Hridaya Sutra* (Great Wisdom Beyond Wisdom Heart Sutra), a distillation of the longer Maha Prajna Paramita Sutra of 100,000 lines. It attempts to explain emptiness, which is the heart, the core of the sutra.

THE MAHA PRAJNA PARAMITA HEART SUTRA

Avalokitesvara Bodhisattva, doing deep prajna paramita,
Clearly saw emptiness of all the five conditions,
Thus completely relieving misfortune and pain.
O Shariputra, form is no other than emptiness,
*   emptiness no other than form;*
Form is exactly emptiness, emptiness exactly form;
Sensation, Conception, Discrimination,
*   Awareness are likewise like this.*
O Shariputra, all Dharmas are forms of emptiness, not born,
*   not destroyed;*
Not stained, not pure, without loss, without gain;
So in emptiness there is no form, no sensation, conception,
*   discrimination, awareness;*
No eye, ear, nose, tongue, body, mind;
No color, sound, smell, taste, touch, phenomena;
No realm of sight . . . no realm of consciousness;
No ignorance and no end to ignorance . . .
No old age and death, and no end to old age and death;
No suffering, no cause of suffering, no extinguishing, no path;
No wisdom and no gain. No gain and thus
The Bodhisattva lives prajna paramita
With no hindrance in the mind, no hindrance, therefore no fear,
Far beyond deluded thoughts—this is nirvana.

All past, present, and future Buddhas live prajna paramita,
And therefore attain anuttara-samyak-sambodhi.
Therefore know, prajna paramita is
The great mantra, the vivid mantra,
The best Mantra, the unsurpassable mantra;
It completely clears all pain—this is the truth, not a lie.
So set forth the Prajna Paramita Mantra,
Set forth this mantra and say:
Gate! Gate! Paragate! Parasamgate!
Bodhi svaha! Prajna Heart Sutra.

This Mahayana scripture did not surface until around the first century A.D. It involves the Buddha talking about Avalokitesvara, the Bodhisattva of Compassion, and her entering into profound wisdom, a wisdom not born of the mind, but the wisdom of life itself—seeing that all things have no permanent identity. For example, in your own experience, are you always the same? When you look, you can see that one moment you are happy, then something happens to change that. You may become angry or indifferent; when you look closer, you may find that you cannot hold onto any aspect of your experience—at the core, you are free and clear. Consider the question, "Where do seeing and hearing arise from?" We don't know the answer. How do we raise the hand? We don't know. Trace any thought or perception back; where do they come from? We don't know. This "not knowing" is vast emptiness. The Heart Sutra says: "All Dharmas (things) are forms of emptiness." Everything arises from emptiness, this unfixed nature. The flip side is true, too. "Emptiness is no other than form." Here you are! You are this Buddha-nature, this emptiness, as you are. So emptiness and form, relative and absolute, intrinsic and experiential, are manifest as the same thing; that is, your momentary experience. In the same way, in Christianity we say that God is in each one of us, and God acts through each one of us, that you can't take God out and yet God cannot be seen as something separate.

Emptiness is often misunderstood in Western culture; people think that Buddhists are trying to blank their minds, that emptiness is blank state. This is a view that could not be further from the truth. The experience of emptiness does not negate anything; rather it embraces everything. Through practice—encountering emptiness and experiencing it—great joy and equanimity is experienced. The experience of emptiness enables us to live from a broader view, one not based on me, I, my desires and wishes, but resting in the direct experience of life, seeing my life and the life of others as one and the same thing.

THE 3 DHARMA SEALS OR MARKS OF EXISTENCE

1.   Impermanence.
2.   Suffering.
3.   No-Self.

According to the Buddhist view, the three Dharma Seals mark the three most important features of life experience. The Buddha proposed that through the study of these three seals of existence, the practitioner is led to an honest and courageous appreciation of life, one that is not dependent on attachment to any fixed set of ideas or values.

1. Impermanence

Impermanence is obvious: most of us today see that we come into this world with nothing, and when we leave we don't take even the corpse. Many people like new things, and feel somewhat sad when they get old. Every bad or difficult situation we have changes, just as every wonderful party has to end. Friends get old and die, babies are born, and new friends come into being. Even mountains erode into the sea, and no moment of our lives is the same as the one before. So it is important to see that this is the nature of our life. When we accept it, we are at peace. If we don't, we are in trouble.

Even society's view of being a successful human being changes. If we aim for this, then we will end up expending a whole load of effort and still find no fixed standard. The constant search for something fixed that will save us is called *samsara* (the wheel of existence). We don't need to be somebody, or have new things to feel good about ourselves. All we need to do is see that life is impermanent. In seeing impermanence, we see there is no need to cover that fact over; it is better to use that energy in understanding the very nature of our existence.

Master Joshu (Joshu Jushin, 778–897) was once asked: "Does a newborn baby have the six consciousness or not?" Joshu said: "It's like throwing a ball in a swift stream." On asking Tosu about this, Tosu replied: "Moment to moment non-stop flow." Focusing on this "moment to moment non-stop flow", whether it's a baby or adult, doesn't matter. With the baby the discriminating faculties are not fully developed, yet consciousness never ceases to flow, not for an instant, even when asleep. At the same time, we cannot grasp consciousness and we cannot freeze time. The past is gone; the future has not arrived. We cannot grasp this present moment. If we try and keep checking where we stand, we lose the flow and our awareness slips into confusion. Even this very consciousness by its nature is impermanent.

2. Suffering (Dukkha)

We suffer because of all kinds of factors: shortage or excess of food or heat, physical and mental pain, misunderstanding life's impermanent nature, and desiring things that are impossible or that we cannot have. Even though it cannot be eliminated, we can do quite a lot to reduce physical distress; yet we suffer the most from misplaced and unfulfillable desires. Popular songs are forever giving us lessons in impermanence and suffering: "I thought you'd love me forever."; "I gave my heart to you and you threw it on the ground." Wanting things to be one way, when really they are another, invites suffering because we are out of sync with the way things are.

3. No-Self

Another facet of emptiness is "no-self" or "the impersonal." The approach here is through understanding what is this "self." As part of his fascicle *Actualizing the fundamental point*, Zen master Dogen (1200–53) says: "To study the Way is to study the self, to study the self is to forget the self...." What is this thing called self anyway? What is it made up of?

When we start to practice, we may ask ourselves the question, "Who am I?" Superficially, we have hundreds of answers: "I am Charles."; "I was born in May."; "I am such and such." But somehow, that doesn't satisfy us on a deeper level, so we try to fix our identity by describing what we do: "I am a carpenter."; "I like Frank Zappa's music." and so on. Still that doesn't reach it; We are still not satisfied. Wherever we look, we cannot encapsulate what this self is; try as we may, we cannot tie it down.

Master Rinzai (Rinzai Gigen, died 866) would say, "There is a man of no-rank coming and going out of the holes in your face. If you haven't seen him yet, look, look." Something hears, smells, tastes, touches, thinks, and sees, but though you try and try you cannot grasp it. The way to really experience this no-self, is to let go of notions, and be immersed in experience.

An old master said: "First empty the cup, then your cup can be filled." Or, as Yasutani Roshi would say: "Be like a blank piece of paper on which anything can be written." This is the man of no-rank, this no-self. Being so, you can truly function freely, entering into any circumstance without the baggage of concepts and prejudice, unhindered by old habits and impulse.

The Four Noble Truths and the Eight-fold Path

As we have already seen, the Buddha found through his work that the understanding and application of the Four Noble Truths and Eight-fold Noble Path was the most effective method of dealing with the human condition and of bringing the mind to peace. He used them as a basic teaching device throughout his life.

The Four Noble Truths
1.   Life is suffering.
2.   There is a cause of suffering.
3.   There is an end to suffering.
4.   The way to end suffering is the Eight-fold Path:

The Eight-fold Path
1. Right view or thought.
2. Right intention.
3. Right speech.
4. Right action or discipline.
5. Right livelihood.
6. Right effort.
7. Right mindfulness.
8. Right samadhi or concentration.

The first truth, life is suffering (dukkha), was discussed in the section on the three Dharma-seals. In summary, we suffer both physically and mentally, but the most profound suffering comes from the misunderstanding of life, and not knowing who we are.

The suffering of the second truth, there is a cause of suffering, is caused by relying on our ideas and concepts. We think that chasing whatever we desire will bring satisfaction. Taking on ideas and philosophies that don't match up with life constantly leaves us dissatisfied, hungry for the truth.

The third truth, there is an end to suffering, tells us that peace, nirvana (which literally means to be quenched, have enough, be satisfied), is possible. This is an essential truth; there is peace of mind, and, what's more, the path to achieve it is laid out for us in the fourth of the noble truths.

The Eight-fold Path

The fourth truth is the Eight-fold Path. The Eight-fold Path illustrates eight aspects of life that, if cultivated, bring peace of mind. Each step on the Eight-fold Path begins with the word "right." In this context, "right" has very little to do with right as opposed to wrong, it has instead the sense of "in accord with reality." The Eight-fold Path is as follows:

1.   Right View or Thought

If the key to right thought is "be in accord with reality," then we must think in accord with reality, or see things as they really are. That way, life is accurately reflected, rather than consisting of hopes and dreams that never quite satisfy us. All of us have ways of coloring reality, formed through habit, impulse, or desire. For example, I may have been beaten up as a kid by a guy named Joe; now, whenever I see someone who looks like him, I immediately feel a similar event is going to occur. So, instead of being open to the situation, I already expect life to be the way I imagine it. We do this over and over until we become confused about what is reality and what is mere projection, when all that is required is to see things as they are.

2.   Right Intention
This follows on directly from right thought as part of the thought-to-action process. Normally, as human beings, we think about something, make the intention to do it, and think about how we can carry it out, then actually do it. Intending to be in be accord with reality, we see how that can be done.

3.   Right Speech
In Sanskrit the word for speech is *vac*, which means "word" or "utterance;" its implication is communication. In this step, it means communicate how reality is, not how you think it should be. If it is cold, then it just is cold, it has nothing to do with how "I" think it is. We often add a moral interpretation, then speak the truth. Be aware of what you say and how you say it.

4.   Right Action (Discipline)
This step follows smoothly from right intention, actually doing something, taking this "right view" into action. Often we procrastinate—"I'll leave it until tomorrow."—but right action always exists where we stand.

5.   Right Livelihood
Extend right action or right view into all aspects of life—work, play, raising the kids, and whatever you are doing throughout the day. In this way, meditation becomes a way of life, existing not just when sitting, but illumining all activities.

6.   Right Effort
Effort must be made in practice, but that effort is not straining. Rather, it is focusing one's energies into illumining where you stand, clarifying your own true nature, not focusing on achieving some state, or on an enlightenment experience that you have dreamed up for the future.

7.   Right Mindfulness
Mindfulness is a common practice in Buddhism. At first one just observes; later, mindful practice is to let go of any sense of an observer, and be totally

involved in one's environment, and whatever one is doing, allowing natural awareness to function freely.

8.   Right Samadhi or Concentration

To be at peace with oneself and the world, it is important not to be distracted by a wandering mind, and it is essential to develop good concentration. The easiest way to develop concentration is through za-zen. Where there is little distraction, it is easy to see how the mind works, and understand how we squander our energy by fantasizing. By doing za-zen, great energy is built up and when focused on clarifying what this life is, our true nature can be directly experienced.

The intention of our practice is to experience Shakyamuni Buddha's realization, "I, all living beings, and the great earth simultaneously attain the way." To experience this is to let go of one's feeling of alienation from other things, and experience the whole world as one's body.

THE PRECEPTS

The precepts are regarded as the core of Buddhism. In fact in the Zen School, the words "Zen" and "Precept" are synonymous. It is said that the precepts are the manifestation of Buddha nature and Zen is the practice/realization of that fact.

The precepts are not just a moral code, but directly express our true nature. They also express how to function, in a way that avoids leaning on rules and regulations, and allows the natural functioning of compassion. The Hinayana view places most emphasis on a moral code; the Buddhayana view, on the expression of our true nature; and the Mahayana, on the natural functioning of compassion.

The precepts in the Zen School arise out of the 247 rules for Theravadan monks and the 400 or so rules for nuns, these rules being the basis of the Vinaya. They were modified somewhat in China, but in Japan they were reduced to 16 precepts. These 16 were regarded as the core of Buddhist life; the rest of the rules, in Japanese monasteries, were created to promote harmony and diligent practice. These 16 precepts are as follows:

The 3 Refuges

1.   I take refuge in the Buddha.
2.   I take refuge in the Dharma.
3.   I take refuge in the Sangha.

The 3 Pure Precepts

1. Cease from evil.
2. Do only good.
3. Do good for others.

The 10 Grave Precepts

1. I vow to refrain from killing.
2. I vow to refrain from stealing.
3. I vow to refrain from sexual misconduct and being greedy.
4. I vow to refrain from telling lies.
5. I vow to refrain from being intoxicated and ignorant.
6. I vow to refrain from talking about other's errors and faults.
7. I vow to refrain from elevating myself and blaming others.
8. I vow to refrain from being stingy, especially with the Dharma.
9. I vow to refrain from indulging in anger and hatred.
10. I vow to refrain from speaking ill of the Buddha, Dharma, and Sangha.

The precepts are a life-long study, and in koan study (see p. 109–111), the precepts come right at the end, when there is enough experience and insight to really internalize them, make them our own. If the precepts are not internalized, we stumble into all kinds of trouble, not seeing clearly our role in events, or the wonder of our true nature.

The 3 Refuges (The core of the precepts)

"I take refuge in the Buddha." Taking refuge in the Buddha doesn't mean worshipping the Buddha. In a very simplistic way it could be understood like that, but really to penetrate this precept you have to understand what "Buddha" means. It means "be awakened," awakened from our own self-created illusions about life. When that is clear, then we take refuge in it—in other words, live it. In the absolute sense, Buddha is this vast emptiness, the unknown that embraces our whole life without a moment's lapse, without anything missing.

"I take refuge in the Dharma." This can be understood as taking refuge in the Buddha's teachings, but what really is the teaching of the Buddha? "I, all living beings, the great earth, simultaneously attain the way." Our life contains the life of everything else, my life, your life, the life of the city, plants, creatures, etc—all one and the same. We have the analogy of Indra's Net, a 3-dimensional net extending infinitely throughout space and time. On each node there is a multifaceted jewel that reflects every other jewel on the net. This shows the mutual interdependence of all things. For example, if someone sneezes in China, it may result in a tornado in Kansas. In the same way that we affect our environment, our environment affects us. To take refuge in the Dharma is to realize the whole universe is my body.

"I take refuge in the Sangha (community)." This means practicing together. The original implication of the word *sangha* was forest. In a forest the trees form a wind break against high winds, giving mutual protection and benefit to all. For a lone tree the protection is absent, and the tree could be damaged. In a practice environment we encourage each other. When one person is enthusiastic we all benefit; when that person is struggling, then we encourage him. On a more profound level, the sangha are those who live in vast emptiness [the Buddha refuge], and experience the interrelationship of all things [the Dharma refuge], harmonizing and seamlessly shifting between these two perspectives.

These three refuges are the intrinsic aspect of Buddhist practice. Next we can examine the activity of the "awakened" life.

The 3 Pure Precepts

"Cease from evil." As Master Dogen commented on this precept, "This is the very source of laws, and rules of all Buddhas." Stop causing yourself and others problems by acting out your own self-centered desires. It makes sense on a deeper level—ceasing from evil is realizing your true nature. Don't cover it up with all kinds of impulse and habit.

"Do only good." Do good deeds that benefit the world.

"Do good for others." See your life and the life of others as one and the same, and act in accord with that.

The 10 Grave Precepts

All of the ten grave precepts arise out of these three pure precepts and these three pure precepts arise out of the three refuges. The ten grave precepts illustrate ten common ways that we misunderstand life and give ten ways to remedy it. For example, Master Bodhidharma, in his commentary on the precept of "I vow to refrain from elevating myself and blaming others," instructs:

Self nature is inconceivably wondrous
In the undifferentiated Dharma,
Not speaking of self and other,
Is called the precept of refraining from
elevating myself and blaming others.

In the first two lines, he shows the reality: our true nature cannot be encapsulated by thought, and is indeed wondrous. The second line indicates the intrinsic aspect of the unity of life. The third and fourth show the problem and the solution. Knowing deep down that myself and others are the same life, still I try to make myself feel better by elevating myself above others and then believe that it is true. Bodhidharma gives the obvious solution: just cut it out, that kind of thinking causes trouble. In its extreme this type of wrong thinking results in racial, class, and interpersonal conflict.

Historically, there are three ways of dealing with the precepts:

1.   The Hinayana View

The Hinayana view involves literal observation of the precepts. If it says don't kill, do not do it. By refraining from these negative acts, we can use that energy for the appreciation of life.

2.   The Mahayana View

Sometimes we are placed in situations where the direct observation of the precepts creates an even worse situation. There is a beautiful story of Master Eisai to illustrate this view. One day, during a 12th-century famine in Japan, a woman came to his temple begging for food for her family. Master Eisai said that the temple had barely enough food for the monks and he could not give her any. They had no money either.

So Master Eisai felt really bad: he wracked his brain trying to find something to give her. Finally, he realized that the temple had some gold leaf to cover an old Buddha image, so he gave this to the woman, knowing that it would be enough money for food for 3 weeks. The treasurer monk witnessed the whole transaction and later came to Master Eisai and said: "Don't you know that you will go to hell for that deed?" (of stealing from the sangha). Master Eisai said: "I know, and I'll enjoy every minute of it." If someone is to starve, would you steal? This is one of the dilemmas we face in life: do we lie to prevent something worse happening?

The key to the Mahayana appreciation is having compassion and reverence for life, not for one's egocentric benefit, by taking full responsibility for one's actions. An active example of this Mahayana view is the Buddha's encouragement of his half-brother Nanda, who was tired of the life of a monk and wanted to return to his beautiful wife. The Buddha, through his supernatural powers, took Nanda to the Heaven of the Thirty-Three Palaces, where he showed Nanda 500 gorgeous pink-footed nymphs. "These nymphs", the Buddha said, "will be yours if you practice diligently." Nanda decided he would do so—compared with these nymphs, his Shakyan girl was

1800 pairs of shoes belonging to the young Japanese schoolgirls who assemble in a Zen Buddhist temple every morning for an hour of prayer.

very ugly. He practiced extremely diligently, yet because of his lusty motives he was widely criticized in the sangha and called a "hireling," a person practicing for a reward. Nanda became so ashamed that he vowed to practice without a goal, and in a short period of time he was profoundly awakened. You could say the Buddha had deliberately tempted him, yet that temptation led to Nanda's awakening.

3.   The Buddhayana View

The Buddhayana view, of "No-separation," is the most difficult to grasp. This is the intrinsic view, as in Master Bodhidharma's commentary, "Self-nature is inconceivably wondrous." If you really experience life this way, being whole and complete, how can there be a problem? Being attached to all kinds of illusion and notions, our own perfect and complete nature is obscured. As with the Mahayana view, this Buddhayana view is often used today as an excuse to do what "I" like.

Each of these views should be studied equally, and applied as much as possible. Without the Buddhayana, the core of Buddhism is lost. Without the Hinayana, the social bond and self-discipline is lost. Without the Mahayana, the true functioning of compassion is lost. The precepts are a lifetime of study. If you think you are maintaining them all, look closer. They are not just a moral code, but rather your momentary experience.

Ahimsa

As a footnote to the precepts, there is the practice of Ahimsa, doing the least harm possible. It is impossible to live without killing—even vegetables live. To walk or breathe kills bugs and microbes, even washing kills all kinds of creatures. Knowing this is the case, not killing wantonly, just taking what we need to live, acknowledges that we live because of the beneficence of other plants and creatures.

This ideal is very much like the Native-American view that all animals and plants are our brothers (equals) and that we shouldn't waste their gifts.

KARMA (Cause and Effect)

Karma is becoming a popular word in the English language: it is found in most modern dictionaries and most people understand what it implies. We have sayings, such as "What goes around, comes around," "If you live by the sword, you die by the sword." Karma is a universal law, yet it doesn't occur as we would like.

Zen monk collecting alms, Tokyo market.

It is said there is karma of 3 periods:

Instant Karma

For example: you steal, you get caught, and you pay for it. This is regarded as the best karma as you pay for it right away and do not have the deed weighing on your mind.

Karma of the intermediate period

You steal and get away with it, and you have to lie to cover it up. Then you compound that lie by covering up over and over, until you get caught. It's not a comfortable existence, having the deed weighing on your mind.

Long-term Karma

Doing something and not getting caught, not even confessing, maybe even dying with it, the karma becomes habitual, ingrained and unconscious. Of course, the same applies to actions that produce good.

The important factor to remember about karma is that, as cause and effect, karma happens now, where we stand. We are the effect of causes from beginningless time, and what we do now affects the whole future. The present moment is the only place you can affect any change.

Karma is often misunderstood these days as fate. This confusion arises out of fixed karma. For example: I am born as a man, at least for a lifetime, I live on planet Earth, and I am white. However, most of our karma is not fixed. Take, for example, health. Someone who was born sickly can often, through diet and exercise, become even stronger than so-called normal people. Depending on your efforts, you can overcome many of the hindrances you have in life. However, cause and effect are dynamic, the effect changing constantly according to the circumstance, the variables being time, place, person, and amount.

THE PATH OF THE BODHISATTVA

The Hinayana ideal is that of the Arhat, who has escaped the wheel of rebirth (samsara). The Mahayana ideal is that of the Bodhisattva, s/he who brings all beings to enlightenment before him/herself. It is embodied in the four vows of the Mahayana:

1.   Living Beings are numberless.
         I vow to free them.
2.   Delusions are inexhaustible.
         I vow to end them.
3.   The teachings [Dharmas] are boundless.
         I vow to master them.
4.   The Awakened [Buddha] Way is unsurpassable.
         I vow to embody it.

These vows acknowledge the fact that we practice in the world, not apart from it, and that each thing is at least as important as ourselves. They seem impossible, yet through practice, it is seen that impossibility just takes a little more time and effort. The beauty of these vows is that there is no resting place when you tackle them, and through their practice we are freed from all kinds of delusions that may have hindered us for years. The teachings are boundless as momentary existence is boundless and the awakened way is unsurpassable, as it is the life of each one of us regardless of country, creed, or color.

SIX PARAMITAS (PERFECTIONS)

Within the Mahayana tradition, the six perfections are a central example of the Buddhist practice of formulating paths toward realization. The word paramita means "reached the other shore," or "go beyond" in the sense of transcending the self-imposed limitations of our ordinary minds. By embodying each of these perfections in our daily lives, we can aspire to achieve this aim.

1.   Dana Paramita – Generosity
2.   Sila Paramita – Discipline
3.   Kshanti Paramita – Patience
4.   Virya Paramita – Energy
5.   Dhyana Paramita – Meditation
6.   Prajna Paramita – Wisdom

These are known as the Six Transcendental Perfections. They enable us to take care of all aspects of life. Giving of time, money, and energy helps in letting go of self-concern and obviously helps others. Without discipline, nothing is accomplished. Practicing patience helps us to appreciate what is apparent now. Through practicing energetically, we wear away hindrances. Through meditation, the illusion of a separate self is abandoned. Thus manifesting wisdom, we benefit all. Most of these Paramitas have been dealt with in this chapter under various titles, but the practice of the Paramitas is a lifetime study in itself.

Buddhism has many teachings; those presented here are the most basic and perhaps the most important. Considered and practiced together in our lives, the intrinsic view, the marks of existence, and Bodhisattva functioning in the world will help us to see through the fabric of our illusions and allow us to experience our innate freedom.

Ch'an in China

T his chapter covers about 1200 years of history, from a little after Christ's death, until around 1250, when many Japanese Zen practitioners went to China to study, and brought Zen back to Japan to stay. The period spans three dynasties in China. The Han Dynasty (206 B.C.–A.D. 220), where Buddhism struggled to get a toe hold in the existing Confucian society, through nearly four centuries of division and invasion to the T'ang Dynasty (618–906), known as the Golden Age of Ch'an (Zen), and the following Sung Dynasty (906–1276), where Ch'an flourished under the umbrella of government support and spread to Korea, Japan, and Vietnam.

To cover this period adequately would take several books; to cover it in one chapter is merely scratching the surface—the references have to be selective and generalizations have to be made. Because of the vast body of literature and the plethora of masters, we will mainly trace the Ts'ao-tsung (Soto) and Lin-chi (Rinzai) lineages from the Golden Age onward. Some famous masters of other lineages will be included because of their effect on Ch'an practice as a whole.

THE EARLY DAYS

By the end of the Ch'in Dynasty (221–207 B.C.) China was forcibly unified and the old feudal system was replaced by a two class system. Chinese civilization was based around the north China plain extending into the Yangtze basin, Pyong yang (Korea), and northern Indo-China, and bordered to the west and north-west by desert and the steppe, and to the north by the Great Wall. Confucianism was adopted as the state religion and manipulated to support the status quo, taking on aspects of Taoism and Chinese philosophy. This system was accepted through all of society and had the effect of limiting thought, so the acceptance of new world views was at first difficult. With the collapse of this system, through corruption, rebellion (including the Yellow Turban Rebellion of A.D. 184 and A.D. 189), famine, and coup d'état, confidence was lost in the old Confucian beliefs, and thoughtful Chinese society began to look for solutions to its problems.

Throughout this period of decline and disintegration, Buddhism was slowly spreading and taking root in scattered centers throughout the empire.

The geographical distribution of these centers suggests that Buddhism spread from the Indo-Iranian and Serindian Kingdoms of Central Asia along the trade routes between those kingdoms and China, then spread through internal routes of trade and communication. Early examples of Buddhist centers are Tun-huang in northwestern China, southern Shantung, and Anhue. Indian traders and sailors brought Buddhism to the southeastern coastal outpost of Chian-chou.

In these early days Buddhism had very little influence on Chinese society as a whole, though it is mentioned in Chinese literature from the first century onward.

THE CULTURE CLASH

Chinese and Indian culture were very different, and they clashed on several important issues. Before Buddhism could be widely accepted, these issues had to be addressed. Indian Buddhist literature tended to be discursive, repetitive, and full of abstraction: Chinese literature was characterized by its familiar metaphors, directness, and concrete imagery. The structure of society was much different from India to China. The Chinese had a strong work ethic, while the rules of the Indian Buddhist Vinaya prohibited monks from working; thus Confucians criticized Buddhists as being economic parasites.

In India even rulers would bow before monks. In China the Emperor was regarded as the first son of China, the living representative of the Ancestors. Chinese civilization would never let the Emperor bow before monks, so a concession was made where monks bowed to the Emperor. Next, the Buddhist view of karma and the Chinese notion that all deceased ancestors went to paradise, were at odds. The Chinese believed that offerings were made to the ancestors to keep them happy and to stop them coming back to cause mischief on this worldly plain. The karmic view was that the ancestors were not necessarily born again as human beings, but rather born where their merit deserved, a shocking belief to the Chinese. A compromise was eventually achieved to let the Buddhist priest make offerings on behalf of the ancestors, so that they might be reborn in better circumstances, a reasonable fee being extracted by the priests for the services. The result? Everybody was happy.

The Confucians repeatedly confronted the Buddhists with the section of the Vinaya forbidding monks to do manual work, calling the Buddhists economic parasites. The Buddhists, by the 3rd century, already had large land holdings with serfs and had a strong economic effect on several regions. As a result of the criticism, the rule in the Vinaya was relaxed enough to satisfy the critics, although there is little evidence that work practice in

Buddhist communities was radically altered. By the 6th century there is evidence that T''ien-tai (Tendai) monks helped to bring in the harvest, and the 8th-century Zen monk Pai-chang (Hyakujo) made statements such as "A day without work is a day without food." Such statements and practices reflect changing attitudes in the Buddhist view on work.

The fundamental change in the acculturation of Buddhism was in the rhetoric, or how Buddhism was made accessible to the masses. Contemporary scholars are now saying that this is what made Ch'an (Zen) different from the standard Buddhist approach. Initially, Zen was not a different school with different facilities and practices. What made Zen masters distinct was their use of common Chinese expression to bring Buddhism alive, through popular idioms that people could understand. Chinese poetry and folklore was used to illustrate Buddhist views. Taoism, being popular at the time, was often blended into expression, and conversely Taoism borrowed freely from Buddhist expression.

It is widely accepted that the Zen school did not fully emerge as a separate school until the 11th century (Sung Dynasty), when government sponsorship of Zen monasteries, which had Zen lineage holders in residence, was available. The major part of this acculturation took around four centuries from the introduction of Buddhism. Many challenges were encountered and overcame as Chinese Buddhism matured.

EARLY CH'AN (ZEN)

The development of the Ch'an (Zen) school can be traced from the 6th century with the first historical figure, Master Bodhidharma, who supposedly brought Dhyana (Ch'an) from India (4th–6th century). Little is known about this great master. Legend has it that, on his arrival in China, he met the Buddhist Emperor Wu of Liang (ruled 502–542). The emperor said "What is the highest meaning of the holy truths?" Bodhidharma said "Vast emptiness, no holiness." The emperor then asked, "What merit have I gained through building several thousand temples, supporting many monks, and donating to many translation projects?" Bodhidharma replied, "No merit." The emperor, a little irate by this point, said, "Who are you to say this?" Bodhidharma retorted, "I know not." Bodhidharma then bowed and left, crossing the Yangtze River to spend nine years facing a wall. During this period a legend says that he became so disgusted with his desire to sleep that he tore off his eyelids and threw them to the floor, and that from these eyelids grew the first tea bushes. He produced five successors, the main successor being Hui-k'o (Taiso Eka, 486–593). Bodhidharma is said to have lived over 150 years, to be the founder of the Shaolin Monastery, and the person who introduced

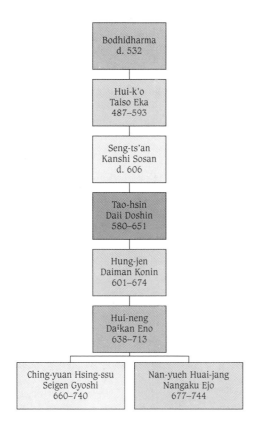

Bodhidharma's Line.

martial arts to China. He introduced kung-fu so that monks could get some exercise and protect themselves from bandits in that region. Little is left of his writings, his commentary on the precepts being the best known. An example of a saying, attributed to him, is this phrase exhibiting the core of Zen:

A special transmission outside the scriptures;
Without dependence on words or letters;
Directly pointing to the mind;
Seeing one's true nature and attaining Buddhahood.

There is little evidence that an historic figure named Bodhidharma existed. Even so, the myth if not the reality of his life has had an important influence on Zen.

Although Zen practice was undeveloped at the time of Bodhidharma, Buddhism was a vital part of Chinese culture, both in the northern and southern regions of divided China. At this point, it is worthwhile mentioning Chih-i (538-97), the founder of Tien-tai Buddhism at this point, as he was a contemporary of Bodhidharma. His systematic classification of Buddhist scriptures explained the many and partially contradictory doctrines of Buddhism. His writings on meditation practice are still used in Chinese and Japanese Buddhism today. The Zen sect borrowed freely from this resource.

Another contemporary of Bodhidharma of note was Mahasattva Fu (Fu Daishi, 497–569). He was a farmer who sold all of his possessions three times during his life, and gave all of the proceeds to the poor. In fact, he hired himself and his family out as day laborers so that the poor could be fed. Like Bodhidharma, he taught Emperor Wu, who seems to have served as a fall guy for these early Zen masters. Fu Daishi and his family serve as excellent examples of lay practice. The following poem shows his depth of understanding and social concern:

The highest good has an empty heart as its basis, and non-attachment as its source; abolishment formality is the cause, and nirvana the result.

The middling good has government of oneself as its basis, and government of the nation as its source; the fruits experienced by gods and humans will be peace and happiness.

The least good is to protect and nourish living beings, to overcome cruelty and abolish murder, and to have all the farmers receive free food six times a month.

Hui-k'o (Taiso Eka) received the Dharma from Bodhidharma and after training a successor himself resumed his lay life, saying that living and teaching in the streets was good for his practice. He was executed in 593, after being falsely accused of misleading the people. His successor Seng-ts'an (Kanshi Sosan) was a leper who wrote a treatise, *The Hsin Hsin Ming* (*Having Faith in Mind*) which is often referred to in Zen literature, and is studied to this day. It begins, "The perfect Way knows no difficulty; it just dislikes choosing. If the slightest like or dislike arises, the mind is lost in confusion."

The fourth Chinese master in the lineage Tao-hsin (Daii Doshin) became a national teacher. His successor Hung-jen (Daiman Konin) passed on the Dharma to Hui-neng. Hui-neng was born in the frontier region of southern China. His father died when he was young, so he was raised by his

mother. They lived in poverty and from a very young age he made a living cutting and gathering wood for sale in the local town. One day, when visiting town, he heard a monk reciting the Diamond Sutra. On hearing "You should activate the mind, not dwelling on anything," he was instantly enlightened. He asked where this phrase came from and the monk said that he learned it from Hung-jen. So he went to visit Hung-jen who, realizing his potential, kept him away from the influence of other monks, having him pound rice for eight months in the rice shed. When Hung-jen was about to die, he asked for poems from the monks expressing their understanding; the writer of the best poem would be chosen as successor. The head monk Shen-hsui wrote:

The Diamond Sutra, *first printed in Chinese* A.D. *400.*

The body is the tree of enlightenment,
The mind is like a bright mirror-stand.
Wipe it clean over and over
and do not let the dust alight.

Hui-neng felt that he could do better. He was illiterate, but managed to persuade a monk to write it for him.

Enlightenment is essentially not a tree;
The bright mirror is not a stand
From the beginning nothing exists;
Where can dust collect?

Hung-jen, being deeply impressed by Hui-neng's poem, had found his successor. At midnight he called in Hui-neng, transmitted the robe and bowl to him (the symbol of transmission), and told him to flee the monastery, as people would be jealous. Hui-neng at that time was still under 20 years old, illiterate, lower class, and what's more, he was a southern barbarian—not even a monk. He followed his teacher's advice and didn't teach for 10 years, living in a town, blending in with the people. Later, he became a monk and settled down to teach. Soon hundreds of people came to study under him, and for the first time the Zen school began to flourish. During his teaching career, he wrote the *Platform Sutra*, another influential text in the Zen tradition. Also during Hui-neng's life, antagonism arose between the Northern School under Shen-hsiu (Hui-neng's Dharma brother), who was a proponent of the gradual school of enlightenment, and the southern school of the followers of Hui-neng, who supported the sudden school of enlightenment. This debate was to continue throughout the history of Chinese Buddhism: is enlightenment suddenly realized or is it realized through practice gradually? Sometimes groups even fought over this.

The T'ang Dynasty began about the time of the Hui-neng's enlightenment. China was once again united and this heralded the Golden Age of Zen.

THE GOLDEN AGE OF ZEN

Hui-neng, the Sixth Ancestor had five major successors and two of them were at the head of the Ts'ao-tung (Soto) and Lin-chi (Rinzai) lineages: Ch'ing-yuan Hsing-ssu (Seigen Gyoshi 660–740) and Nan-yueh Huai-jang (Nangaku Ejo 677–744) respectfully.

The personalities of Hsing-ssu and Huai-jang were very different. Hsing-ssu was more taciturn, enjoyed quiet sitting, and wasn't fond of public speaking. Huai-jang, on the other hand, had more of a public persona and enjoyed actively engaging in the world. They tended to attract like-minded people, so differences in practice arose.

An example of Hsing-ssu (Seigen) understanding is shown in one of the first recorded dialogues between Hui-neng and Hsing-ssu. Hsing-ssu asked, "What should I do so as not to land in some class or stage?" Hui-neng asked, "What have you done so far?" Hsing-Ssu replied, " I have not even tried the four

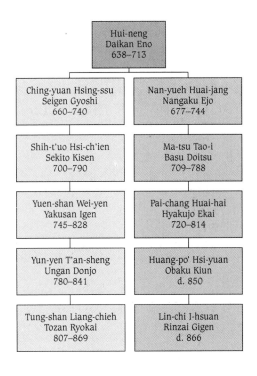

noble truths." Hui-neng asked "In what stage will you end up?" "If I still have not tried the four noble truths, what stage can there be?" Hui-neng was greatly impressed with his potential.

Hsing-ssu had deep faith in his own realization. For him it was a living reality and not contingent on circumstances or method. He had only one successor, Shih-t'ou Hsi-ch'ien (Sekito Kisen, 700–790). Master Shih-t'ou was an excellent master who began studying with the sixth ancestor Hui-neng. When Hui-neng died, he was sent by Huai-jang (Nangaku) to Hsing-ssu. After succeeding Hsing-ssu, his influence spread throughout China and he produced many enlightened successors. His contemporary Ma-tsu would often send students his way and vice versa, both appreciating each other's teaching methods and realization. In fact, Shih-Tou's successor Yaoshan attained enlightenment under Ma-tsu. Shih-tou is famous for his verse *The Identity of Relative and Absolute*, which is chanted today in Zen monasteries all over the world.

In the third generation after Shi-t'ou, the great master Tung-shan Liang-chieh (Tozan Ryokai, 807–869) emerged. The co-founder along with Ts'oa-shan Pen-chi (Sozan Honjaku, 840–901) of the Ts'oa-tung (Soto) line, Tung-shan had tremendous ability and studied with several highly reputable masters, including Nan-ch'uan (Nansen) and Kuei-shan (Isan). Tung-shan came to realization while seeing his reflection when crossing a stream. He described it in verse thus:

Avoid seeking him in someone else
or you will be far apart from the self.
Solitary now am I, and independent,
but I meet him everywhere.
He now is surely me,
but I am not he.
Understanding it in this way,
you will directly be one with thusness.

His work on the five ranks, or positions in practice, has become an essential part of koan practice in both the Soto and Rinzai schools. He is also the author of the *Jeweled Mirror Samadhi* (Jap. Hokyo Zanmai). Tozan's line has often been called the lineage of "Meticulous Study of the Principle" because of its emphasis on thorough practice, realization, and the actualization of the enlightened way.

Going back to Nan-yueh Huai-jang (Nangaku Ejo), we can trace the beginnings of the Rinzai line. Although Huai-jang was an excellent master, he is somewhat overshadowed by his successor Ma-tsu Tao-i (Baso Doitsu, 709–788), who had 120 enlightened successors. The following dialog illustrates the style of these masters:

One day, Ma-tsu was sitting alone in meditation and master Huai-jang said, "What are you doing?" Ma-tsu said, "I'm sitting to become Buddha." Huai-jang picked up a tile and began polishing it. Ma-tsu said, "What are you doing?" Huai-jang said, "I'm polishing this tile, so that it will become a mirror." "You can't do that," exclaimed Ma-tsu. Huai-jang replied, "In the same way you cannot make a mirror through polishing a tile, you cannot become a Buddha through sitting." Ma-tsu said, "What should I do then?" Huai-jang said, "Take the case of an ox cart. Do you whip the ox or the cart, if the cart does not move?" Ma-tsu remained silent. "In learning sitting-in-meditation, do you aspire to learn the sitting Zen, or do you aspire to imitate the sitting Buddha? If the former, Zen is not restricted to sitting or lying down. If the latter, the Buddha has no fixed postures. The Dharma goes on forever and never abides in anything. Therefore you must not be attached to, or abandon any particular phase of it. To sit yourself into Buddha is to kill the Buddha. To be attached to the sitting posture is to fail to comprehend the essential principle."

With this active teaching the Huai-jang line flourished, first under Ma-tsu Tao-i (Baso Doitsu), then through Pai-chang Huai-hai (Hyakujo Ekai, 720–814). Pai-chang apparently was a great organizer, tough and very thorough; he is regarded as the person who first formulated monastic rules and applied them to his sangha. Nothing remains of these rules, yet they are referred to in other monastic codes. Pai-chang continued Ma-tsu's vigorous training and produced two great Dharma heirs, Kei-shan Ling-yu (Isan Reiyu, 771–853) and Huang-po Hsi-yuan (Obaku Kiun, died 850). Both were unwitting founders of Zen lines. Huang-po is said to have been seven feet tall and had a bump on his head; some say this was caused by bowing, others say it was congenital. His successor Master Lin-chi I-hsuan (Rinzai Gigen, died 866), was only a small man, yet in recorded anecdotes he didn't seem to be intimidated by Huang-po's giant size. In the *Record of Lin-chi*, there are several examples of vigorous exchange between the two.

Once, during community work, Lin-chi was hoeing the ground. Seeing Huang-po coming, he stopped and stood leaning on his mattock. "Is this man tired already?" said Huang-po.

"I haven't even lifted my mattock yet, how could I be tired?" answered Lin-chi. Huang-po hit at him. Lin-chi seized Huang-po's stick, jabbed him with it, and knocked him down.

Huang-po called to the work leader, "Help me up!" The work leader came running and helped him up. "Master, how can you let this lunatic get away with such rudeness?" he said. No sooner had Huang-po got to his feet than he hit the work leader.

Later Kuei-shan asked Yang-shan: "What did Huang-po have in mind when he hit the work leader?" "The real thief escapes, and his pursuer gets the stick," answered Yang-shan.

Master Rinzai is famous for the "stick and the shout" methods of skilful means. Although later masters criticize him for the rough use of the "stick and shout", this was the earlier phase of his teaching. Later on, his teaching matured and exhibited subtlety rivaling the best masters.

Here's a quotation from the tenth talk of the *Record of Lin-chi*. It shows his vigorous approach.

Students today can't get anywhere: what ails you? Lack of faith in yourself is what ails you. If you lack faith in yourself, you'll keep tumbling along, bewilderedly following after all kinds of circumstances, be taken by these myriad circumstances through transformation after transformation, and never be yourself. Bring to rest the thoughts of the ceaselessly seeking mind, and you'll not differ from the Buddha. Do you want to know the Buddha? He is no other than you who stand before me listening to my discourse... .

So far the pre-Ts'ao-tung (Soto) and Lin-chi (Rinzai) lines have been illustrated. It was easy to visit masters of other lineages. Some even received succession from two masters of different lines—for example, Layman P'ang (whose quotation "How miraculous, how wonderful! I draw water, I carry wood" is in the introduction, p. 8) succeeded both Ma-tsu and Shih-tou. Sectarian lines did not solidify until the Meiji period (1850) in Japan. Obviously, there have always been preferences for one line or the other, yet if a master was skillful he would draw students from any lineage.

THE FIVE HOUSES OF ZEN

In the Five Houses, the Lin-chi (Rinzai) and Tsao-tung (Soto) lines are major branches that have continued to this day, yet there are three more that have had a major influence on Zen practice. The oldest house or line was the Kei-yang (Igyo) line, which lasted until the early part of the Sung dynasty. The Igyo line was a close relation to the Lin-chi line, sharing the common ancestor Pai-chang (Hyakujo). Pai-chang's successor Kuei-shan (Isan, 771–853) and his successor Yang-shan (Kyozan, 807–883) were its founders, the first parts of their names forming the lineage name. The family style was "two mouths with one tongue," indicating the intimate relationship between teacher and student. Another teaching device they employed was using 97 circles to illustrate stages of enlightenment.

The Fa-yen (Hogen) and Yun-men (Ummon) schools are offshoots of Shih-tou's pre-Soto line (see lineage chart on page 63.) Master Wen-yen of Yun-men (Ummon Bun'en, died 949), a successor of Hsueh-feng I-ts'un (Seppo Gison, 822–908), forbade his students to record his sayings, though fortunately one of his students recorded them on a paper robe. He extensively used the sayings of the old masters in Dharma dialog and added substitute answers for speechless monks, alternative answers to old sayings. Sometimes he would pose his own questions to these old cases, and his answers often had three levels of meaning. Ummon was the first of the Zen masters to extensively use these techniques. His line continued into the 13th century and was responsible for the koan collection the *Blue Cliff Record*.

Master Fa-yen Wen-i (Hogen Mon'eki, 885–958) was a third generation successor of Hsueh-feng, Yun-men's teacher. His line continued for five generations, about one hundred years. The family style was that of "two arrow points meeting"; when a question is asked, it is met accurately, head-on.

Before moving to the Sung dynasty, we must mention several masters of high repute who have influenced successive generations until today. The first master, Nan-chu'an (Nansen) was the primary successor of Ma-tsu, and his teachings had a marked effect on Buddhist practitioners of the day. His

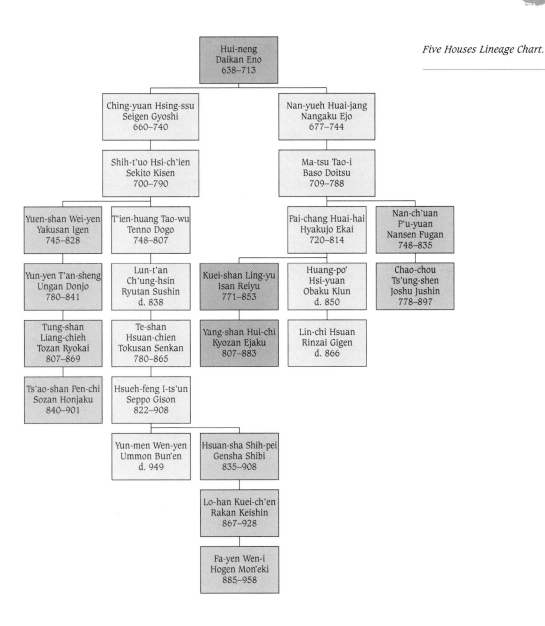

Five Houses Lineage Chart.

successor Chao-chou Ts'ung-shen (Joshu Jushin, 778–897), was a prime example of mature practice, having his first enlightenment experience at the age of eighteen. His practice matured for a further 40 years until his teacher Nan-ch'uan died. Chao-chou (Joshu) was about 60 at the time, but after three years of mourning (a tradition in China), Chao-chou (Joshu) set out on pilgrimage. His attitude was remarkable. He made a vow, "If I can teach an eighty-year-old man who doesn't understand the way, I will teach him. If a seven-year-old girl has something to teach me, I will learn." Having such an open attitude, he traveled around China seeing many famous masters of that era. At the age of 80 he settled down to teach and taught until he was 120 years old. His reputation was impeccable; Master Dogen, one of the 13th century's great masters, called him "old Buddha," so impressed was he by Chao-chou's teaching. In Zen literature he is known as the "Golden tongue Buddha." Many of Chao-chou's (Joshu's) dialogs are used today, including *Mu*.

A monk asked Chao-chou in all earnestness, "Does a dog have Buddha-nature?" Chao-chou in reply said, "Mu."

This is quite often the first koan in formal koan study and illustrates Chao-chou's realize-it-for-yourself attitude. His dialogs range from direct one word or one sentence responses, through profound imagery, to ridiculous humor. Unfortunately, his lineage died out.

Hsueh-feng I-ts'un (Seppo Gison, 822–908), experienced realization in his 40s after studying for twenty years prior to that. He traveled around as a *tenzo* (cook) from temple to temple. When he settled down, he had a monastery of over 1500 monks and many excellent successors including Yun-men, Ch'ang-ch'ing, Ching-ch'ing, Ts'ui-yen, and Hsuan-sha Shih-pei. The latter, Hsuan-sha Shih-pei (Gensha Shibi, 835–908), earned his living as a fisherman alongside his father. One day his father was washed overboard and drowned. Hsuan-sha searched for him, but his beloved father was lost. Returning to port, he went straight to Hsueh-feng's monastery and practiced with such intensity that he was enlightened within three years. His insight and expression were profound; here are a couple of his phrases:

The whole world is one bright pearl.
Shakyamuni and I practiced together.

A monk asked, "Who did you practice with?" Hsuan-Sha replied, "Shakya Muni and I practiced together." "Then who did you practice with?" "With the third son of Zhe on a fishing boat," replied Hsuan-sha, Hsuan-sha being the third son of Zhe. Two generations later, Master Fa-yen (Hogen) revived Hsuan-sha's (Gensha's) line.

SUNG CHINA 906–1276

In the Sung dynasty, the Ch'an (Zen) practice became widespread and the notion of a separate Zen sect became reality. Although there were many great masters in this period, very few received the notoriety of the Golden Age. The

The Great Buddha, Da fo si, in the Zhao qing si Temple, Hanchow, rebuilt in the 20th century, but no longer used. The original Buddha was carved out of stone in the 12th century.

Ts'ao tung (Soto) line declined somewhat, and was rescued by a Lin-chi (Rinzai) master, Fushin, after the death of Liang-shan Yüan-kuan (Ryozan Enkan), successor in the Ts'ao-tung line. Fushin, Liang-shan's friend was asked to pass on the Ts'ao-tung lineage to someone demonstrating a profound realization and possessing Ts'ao-tung's understanding. Fushin found T'ou-tzu I-ch'ing (Tosu Gisei, 1032–1083), and the lineage was saved.

The Rinzai lineage went through its ups and downs and produced several great masters in the 11th and 12th centuries, including Yuan-wu K'o-ch'in (Engo Kokugon), Ta-hui Tsung-Kao (Daie Soko), and Wu-men Hui-k'ai (Mumon Ekai, 1183–1260). At the start of the Sung dynasty, the Lin-chi school split into two separate lines, the Oryu and Yogi. The Oryu school continued until the 13th century, and died out with Master Eisai in 1215, Dogen Kigen's Rinzai teacher in Japan. Master Dogen inherited both lines of Soto and Rinzai.

The Yogi school produced at least two lines which survived into Japan, on through Shinji Kakushin (1207–1298) and Sung-yüan Ch'ung-yueh (Shogen Sugaku, 1139–1209), the latter line going all the way through to Master Hakuin Ekaku, 1685–1768, who formulated modern koan study.

KUNG-AN (KOAN) AND SHIKANTAZA

These two common approaches to practice are best exhibited in the Rinzai and Soto lines. Kung-an (koan) literally means "public case." Just as government declarations (kung-an) were posted for all to see, one's life becomes open to the life of everything else. This is achieved through basic questions about life or the stories of the ancient masters, realizing their meaning and embodying that without a doubt.

When koans were first used, they arose out of circumstance—for example, "What is the nature of the wind?" This approach was easy while the communities were small. When teachers began having many students, common public cases (koans) were used to stimulate students' efforts and bring them to realization.

The first effort to gather koans into one collection was by Nan-yuan Hui-yung (Nan'in Egyo, d. 930), a third-generation successor of Master Lin-chi. He was the first to systematize Master Lin-chi's teaching formulas.

Later, again in the Lin-chi (Rinzai) line, Master Fen-yang Shan-chao (Fun'yo Zensho, 947–1024) became the first to add his own comments to his koan collection. This collection of three volumes of 100 koans each became a model for the future koan collections.

Just after the turn of the 11th century, Master Hsueh-tou Ch'ung-hsien (Setcho Juken, 980–1052), a master in the Yun-men (Ummon) line, compiled the Pi Yen Lu (Hekigan Roku) *Blue Cliff Record*—a collection of 100 koans, to which he added verses and additional remarks of his own. About 60 years after Hsueh-tou's (Setcho's) death, the Lin-chi Master Yuan-wu K'e-ch'in (Engo Kokugon, 1063–1135), got hold of this collection and added remarks and commentaries. Yuan-wu's successor Ta-hui Tsung-kao (Daie Soko, 1089–1163), known as the second Rinzai, burned the printing blocks of this book when he felt people were beginning to cling to the text rather than experience its meaning. Ta-hui's (Daie Soko's) good friend, Hung-chih Cheng-chueh (Wanshi Shogaku, 1091–1157), a Dharma successor of Tanka Shijun in the Ts'ao-tung (Soto) lineage, compiled a koan collection called the Ts'ung-jung-lu (Shoyo Roku), *Book of Serenity*, named after the Hut of Serenity he was living in at the time.

These latter two masters optimized the opposing approaches to practice of the time. The koan (kan hua or kanna) Zen story contemplation was advocated by Ta-hui (Daie Soko). The method of koan was to penetrate the story to its essence, or embody the story until its essence is revealed. The "Mo-jiao" (Mokusho Zen) or silent illumination practice, later known as shikantaza, "just sitting" was advocated by Hung-chih (Wanshi Shogaku). Shikantaza has been descried as "quiet sitting in open awareness, reflecting directly the reality of life." Both masters openly criticized the other's teaching, yet never questioned the other's attainment. Masters Tahui and Wanshi reveled in keeping their students off-balance, making them rely on their own experience, not the words of their teachers.

Both methods can be criticized, and have been to the present day—

koan Zen for its tendency toward intellectualism, and shikantaza for its tendency toward quietism and dullness. Both approaches are important, koan for clarifying doubt and penetrating to the essence, shikantaza for its experience of living reality.

Both Hung-chih and Ta-hui did much to revive their lines of Zen. Japanese Master Dogen (1200–53) was greatly influenced by these two masters, often criticizing their work to illustrate practice.

Hung-chih's *Book of Serenity* broke from the stereotype of "shikantaza only" in the Soto school. Contrary to popular belief, koan were often used to guide students in the Soto line at this time. It was only later in Japan, where sectarianism raised its ugly head, that koan study in the Ts'ao-tung (Soto) lineage declined.

THE TRANSITION FROM CHINA TO JAPAN

Around the turn of the 13th century, several famous Japanese Masters visited China and returned as successors in the Ts'ao-tung (Soto) and Lin-chi (Rinzai) lines. Eisai returned as a master in the Oryu Lin-chi (Rinzai) line after studying at Mt. T'ien-tong. Dogen studied with Eisai and his successor Myozen, but not being fully satisfied with his own accomplishment, he visited China to study at the same T'ien Tong (Rinzai) monastery as Eisai. At that time, there happened to be a Ts'ao Tung (Soto) abbot in residence, Tientong Ju-ching (Tendo Nyojo), from whom Dogen inherited the Dharma. While he was there, he copied the *Blue Cliff Record* in one night and brought it back to Japan.

Shinji Kakushin returned from China in that same period. He was a Lin-chi (Rinzai) successor from Wu-men Hui-k'ai (Mummon Ekai, 1183–1260), and author of the now-famous *Wu-men Kuan (Mumon Kan)*, a collection of 50 koans widely in use today. Unfortunately, his line died out. The majority of Lin-chi lines in Japan today are of the Yogi line through Yuan-wu (Engo) and Sung-yuan (Shogen Sugaku.)

The Soto lines in China died out in the 17th century, many Ch'an (Zen) lines being absorbed into the Pure Land and other branches of Buddhism. Nowadays the Ch'an of Sung dynasty China tends to be overshadowed by the Ch'an of the Masters of the T'ang dynasty. In reality, however, much of the literature extolling the virtues of T'ang dynasty Zen was written by Sung Masters, and their work was in fact as important as that of the Masters of Golden Age.

It was in China that Zen developed into the fully mature religion it is today, and many of the Chinese forms are still intact in the West. The Chinese legacy was to leave an approach so flexible and accommodating that it is easy for Zen to adapt to new cultures while still preserving its essence.

The History of Zen in Japan

A statue of Buddha seated on a lotus flower from the Muromachi period, 1392–1568.

At the end of the 12th century, Japan underwent a fundamental shift in the balance of political power, which facilitated a renaissance in its Buddhist religion. Before that time Zen, which is often thought of as synonymous with Japanese Buddhism, was not taught or practiced in any distinctly sectarian or formal way. However, the country did have a 600-year-old Buddhist culture, under which large and wealthy monastic institutions had developed. The influence of those institutions on Japanese society had not been entirely benign, and by the 12th century the spiritual integrity of the Buddhist priesthood was seriously undermined. Accomplished teachers of the Dharma were hard to find in any of the great temple complexes. People with any real depth of religious inclination were either breaking away from the established sects, or journeying to China in search of fresh inspiration.

Until 1192 the seat of Japanese government was sited at Heiankyo (modern Kyoto). In 794 it had been relocated there by the Emperor Kammu (737–806) as part of a desperate effort to distance his court from the unwanted interference of the powerful monasteries of the first Imperial capital, Nara.

Early Japanese Buddhism was closely associated with the nation's aristocracy. This was unremarkable in itself. Throughout its history, monastic Buddhism had been patronized by kings, courtiers, and merchants. The monasteries were centers of secular as well as spiritual learning. Their priests provided employment, built roads, schools, and hospitals, and lent cultural sophistication to emergent kingdoms whose civilizations were measured by the number and size of the Buddhist monasteries and temples they sponsored.

The introduction of Buddhism to Japan is attributed to the Imperial Regent Shotoku Taishi (574–662). Although a devout Buddhist, at least part of his motivation for promoting this foreign religion was political and economic. The Imperial family wanted to forge a nation able to rival the civilization, political might, and economic prestige of its Chinese and Korean neighbors. Although the ethnic Shinto beliefs provided a set of shamanistic myths about the origin of the Japanese people and their sacred islands, its inherent pantheism and the close association of its various deities with particular holy places tended to make people provincial in their loyalties, and encouraged rivalry between neighboring clans. If anything, Shinto was seen by the Imperial family as an obstacle to the development of centralized government. The universal values of Mahayana Buddhism were used to turn the (local) Shinto gods into protectors of the (state) Buddha-Dharma. In Nara, Buddhist priests soon found many wealthy patrons, who measured both their prestige at Court and their virtue by the extent to which they gave land and economic subsidy to the monks for the construction of imposing temple complexes. The Buddha Hall at the temple of Todaiji, the world's largest wooden building, was constructed during this epoch, and was a highly visible symbol of Japan's burgeoning nationhood. The Emperor Shomu (724–49) made a direct parallel between his own position as head of state, and that of the image of the Buddha, Dianichi Nyorai, set up in the Todaiji Buddha Hall. Just as the Emperor was the embodiment of all the Japanese peoples, so Dianichi Buddha was the embodiment of the universal Buddha Nature inherent in all beings. However, a combination of reforms in land ownership and taxation, which favored the monasteries, meant that between 710 and 794 the main temples of Nara became increasingly influential in matters of politics and economy, in which they ought to have had no direct interest at all. These religious centers gradually degenerated as prominent monks became more and more interested in political intrigue and the pursuit of private wealth. Matters reached a scandalous climax, and precipitated the move of the capital to Heiankyo, when a leading priest, called Dokyo, seduced the Empress Koken (718–70) and attempted through her to manipulate the reigns of government for his own purposes!

The shift of the Imperial Court also coincided with an attempt at reform in Japanese Buddhism. A visionary monk named Saicho (769–822), disgusted at the state of institutional Buddhism, and inspired by the stories of the yamabushi, the mountain ascetics of indigenous Shinto folklore, sequestered himself in meditation on Mount Hiei and later went to China in search of genuine Buddhist practice. On his return to Japan, the Emperor authorized him to found a new sect, called Tendai, and a training center on Hiei. It was at the foot of Mount Hiei that the Emperor also decided to build the new capital of Heiankyo.

In its early years, Saicho's new Tendai school was a center of strong Buddhist practice. It reinvigorated the study of the Dharma in Japan by placing a fourfold emphasis on meditation (zen), pure doctrine as expounded in the White Lotus Sutra (*engyo*), tantric initiations (*tai-mitsu*), and the precepts (*kai*). The Tendai doctrines stressed the universal accessibility of Buddha Nature at the expense of the ecclesiastic hierarchy of Nara, and therefore the new sect was immensely popular with the laity.

Unfortunately, the religious purity of the Tendai sect did not last. The Imperial Court, having escaped the malign influence of the temples of Nara, now fell under the direct shadow of Hiei. The Tendai monks themselves became embroiled in a dispute over the succession to the title of head of the school and, over time, the monks of Hiei became every bit as worldly as were their neighbors in Nara.

By the mid-12th century, the factional disagreements within the Tendai school had deteriorated to the point of outright hostility. Buddhist temples, including many on and around Hiei, terrorized the populace by the combined deployment of occult tantra and private armies! It was the role of so-called warrior-monks, the sohei, to burn down rival temples and generally remind the Court where the real political power lay. The Emperor Shirakawa (1053–1129) had good cause to lament that, even though he ruled all Japan and could claim descent from the Shinto Goddess of the Sun, there were three things beyond his control: the roll of a dice, the flood waters of the River Kamu, and the monks of Mount Hiei! Politically and militarily, the Court had lost control.

In the realm of religion, the problem for anyone at the end of the 12th century with an aspiration to raise the *Bodhicitta*, the Way-seeking mind, was the very dominant position occupied by the decadent institutional monasteries and their militant warrior-monks. Within the mountain fortress of Hiei, there were over 3,000 temple buildings, the influence of whose malevolent priests seemed to extend into every area of the life of the capital. Travel of any distance would have been hazardous and, in any event, the temples in other parts of the country were, by reputation, no better and in some cases perhaps worse, than they were on Hiei. Japanese Buddhism was in desperate need of fresh vision. As a great master of later years was to remark caustically, the teachers on Hiei counseled the study of Buddhist doctrine until pupils knew as much as their teachers, only so that they could then make themselves known in the capital and gain fame at Court.

It was in the midst of this melting pot of questionable spiritual practice and factional in-fighting that a few Tendai priests, who were genuinely worthy of their Buddhist robes, gained permission to travel abroad in search of new teachings. One of them, Myoan Eisai (1141–1215), is generally regarded as the first fully certified Japanese Zen master. He journeyed to China in 1168, and again during the years 1187–91. It was on the second visit that he entered a Ch'an monastery and there encountered zazen and koan for the first time. Eisai was evidently a Zen student of considerable capacity because at the end of this second short sojourn in China he received the transmission of the Dharma in the Lin-chi, or Rinzai, sect and was authorized to teach in Japan by Ch'an master Xuan Huaichang (dates unknown).

Not doubting the importance of Zen training as the essence of the Buddha's realization and the means to regenerate Japanese Buddhism, Eisai founded training centers, first at Shofukuji in 1191 on the southern island Kyushu and then in 1202 at Kenninji in Heiankyo and Jufukuji in Kamakura. In accordance with the Rinzai method, he began to encourage students in the disciplined practice of zazen, bringing them to spiritual awakening through the use of koan. However, he did not forsake his early Tendai training. He remained, nominally at least, a Tendai monk, and saw no contradiction between the original teachings of Saicho and the new Zen system. He taught Zen in the context of Saicho's fourfold method, and to the end of his life continued to give Tendai initiations. Eisai was diplomatic and worked to avoid coming into open conflict with the priesthood on Mount Hiei, against whose military might he was helpless anyway. However, his compromise with Hiei was not without benefit. It eased the way for a senior Tendai priest to refer to him a promising young man who would go on to become one of the greatest Zen masters and most original of Japanese religious thinkers.

In 1214 Dogen Kigen (1200–1253) was a 14-year-old Tendai monk. He had studied Tendai doctrine, but was consumed by doubt on one point: if, as the Sutras say, all beings are intrinsically enlightened, why is it necessary to train so hard to realize it? None of Dogen's teachers on Hiei could answer this question for him, yet they felt able to refer him to Eisai, whose radical new approach might, they reasoned, put the young monk's mind to rest. Eisai listened to Dogen, and then cut right through his question:

The Buddhas of the three ages pay no heed to the Buddha-nature, but cats and oxen are only too aware of it!

The meaning was that deluded sentient beings are in bondage, and strive for liberation; the enlightened, on the other hand, because they are enlightened, make no distinction between bondage and liberation, and do not give the matter a second thought. Profoundly struck by this answer, Dogen resolved to train under master Eisai. Sadly, though, this was possible for only a short time. Within a year Eisai died. Nevertheless, there can be no doubt of Eisai's inspirational importance in Dogen's development. In later years Dogen would recall, with great reverence and affection, anecdotes from the life of this first Japanese Zen master. In the *Shobogenzo Zuimonki*, Dogen is recorded as telling his students the tale of Eisai's irreverence for the gold leaf that had been set aside to make a halo for the Temple's Buddha image. It was the only item of value at Kenninji at the time. When a destitute family asked the temple for help, Eisai showed no compunction in giving them the metal, much to the consternation of his students, upon whom he then rounded for their lack of compassion! On another occasion, Dogen recounted how the monks of Kenninji had worried that rising flood waters from the nearby river would destroy the temple. Eisai had quickly put them in their place. The destruction of the temple was inevitable at some time, he said. It was the practice of the Way then and there that was alone important.

Eisai's lineage eventually died out after his death and the Rinzai school developed through several different lines; however, one of his immediate successors Myozen (1184–1225) had a considerable impact on Dogen. Dogen believed Myozen to be without equal and trained with him for nine more years after Eisai's death. In the *Shobogenzo Bendowa* (*On the endeavor of the Way*), Dogen says that under Myozen he understood a little of the Rinzai teachings (in fact, he completed the Rinzai training then available in Japan), but was still left with the doubts of his youth. So it was that in 1223 Dogen embarked on the hazardous voyage to Sung China in search of a complete understanding of the Buddha-Dharma.

Dogen was greatly impressed by the importance the Chinese monks placed on tasks that he would otherwise have regarded as menial and without spiritual content. He explained in his *Tenzo Kyokun* (*Instructions to the Chief Cook*) that the position of cook in a Chinese Zen monastery was one given only to accomplished monks and that the work of preparing a meal was treated with the care and attentiveness normally reserved by Japanese monks for ceremonies and meditation. In China, Dogen's appreciation of what was truly Zen practice changed radically. So too, under Chan master Tie-tung Ju-ching (1163–1228), he came to realize the true meaning of Buddhist Enlightenment. For Dogen, the experience of the Great Awakening to the pristine Buddha mind was what Rujing called "body and mind dropped off." Very simply, this might be understood as the intrinsic unity of everything one would normally think of as polarized or in opposition: self and other, delusion and enlightenment, practice and realization, sentient being and Buddha, and so on. This realization came to him one day when Rujing scolded the monk seated beside him for dozing during zazen. With all personal doubt resolved, and the complete approval of Master Rujing, Dogen returned to Kenninji in 1227, a fully empowered teacher in the Caodong (Soto) Zen sect. According to Dogen:

> **I realized clearly that my eyes are set horizontally and my nose vertically. I returned to Japan without carrying a single sutra. So I have no Buddhism.**

He stayed at his old temple for three years and there wrote the *Fukan Zazenji* (*Universal Recommendation of the Practice of Za-zen*) which is a comprehensive treatise on Shikantaza, "just sitting," the meditation method of Soto Zen which Dogen was to promote above all else. By so doing, he clearly separated himself from Eisai's other successors, who continued to teach Tendai mixed practices. Later, Dogen moved to Koshoji on the outskirts of the Hieankyo where he began the composition of his monumental *Shobogenzo* (*Treasury of the True Dharma Eye*). This religious masterpiece, which would eventually run to 95 fascicles and cover the range of Dogen's genius, was not compiled until his untimely death in 1253. It is one of the treasures of Japanese literature. At Koshoji, Dogen built Japan's first *Sodo*, a single training hall in which monks eat, sleep, and practice zazen.

Dogen was outspoken in his criticism of what he regarded, with some justification, as the deplorable state of Buddhism in Japan, and resisted the patrimony of rich and powerful families. He was demanding of his students, imposing on them a rigorous training regime. He wanted only practitioners with a pure aspiration to accomplish what he called the Great Matter. As the number of his followers grew, so too did his own reputation as a true follower of the Way. Inevitably, perhaps, he drew the wrath of the priesthood on Hiei, who according to one version of events ordered the destruction of Koshoji, forcing Dogen and his followers to flee the capital.

In 1244 Dogen founded a new Soto Zen training center called Eiheiji in the remote province of Echizen. Far removed from the mainstream of political life and free from the persecution of the old monastic institutions, the new Soto Zen sect was able to pursue the undistracted and intensive practice of zazen. On his death, Dogen was succeeded as Abbot of Eiheiji by

Ejo (1198–1280), another very able ex-Tendai monk and close disciple after 1234. Ejo was responsible for the compilation of the *Shobogenzo Zuimonki* collection of Dogen's informal talks and it is said that Dogen wrote the *Shobgenzo Bendowa* specifically for him.

Meanwhile, through other followers of Eisai, such as Shoichi Kokushi (1201–1280), who made a seven-year pilgrimage to China in 1235 and founded the Rinzai temple of Tofukuji, Zen became increasingly accepted by society at large for the disciplined meditation practice of its students.

However, for the emergence of Soto and Rinzai Zen as distinct schools, popular acceptance had to be endorsed by official sanction. The Imperial Court at Heiankyo, dominated as it was as it was by the Tendai priests, could not have given it. Fortunately for the new Zen schools, in the second half of the 12th century, political power shifted dramatically into the hands of a new social class known to history as the Samurai.

The Buddhist monasteries had not been alone in taking advantage of the tax and land reforms of earlier centuries. Lesser nobles who had been blocked from personal advancement in the capital had slowly built up provincial estates, private incomes, and large, private armies based on the extended clan loyalties which the Imperial family had originally tried to undermine. In the epoch from 710 to 1180, the Emperors ceded all but the trappings of power to the aristocratic families of the Court, who in turn had become progressively more self-absorbed by the pre-occupations of Court life. As the belligerence of the monasteries grew into open conflict during the 12th century, the Court turned for help to the armies of the provincial nobles upon whom they became increasingly dependent to keep the peace. Finally, through a series of battles between 1156 and 1185, the two most powerful military families, the Taira and the Minamoto, found themselves in a position to seize the reigns of government for themselves. At first, the Taira took control of the Imperial family, but after a four-year war Minamoto Yoritomo (1147–1199) established overall military control of the country in 1185 and, in 1192, moved the center of political power to Kamakura. Under Minamoto leadership the country had a new, military head of state called the Shogun. The Samurai, the new dominant class, were to control every aspect of Japanese society until 1868.

The new rulers in Kamakura looked for new vehicles through which to give cultural and religious legitimacy to their political aspirations. As well as Zen, the Nichiren, Jodo, and later the Jodo-shin Buddhist sects had emerged out of the religious decay in the old institutions. In all these new schools, religious zeal and experience were valued above dogma. However, it was Zen in particular which impressed Japan's strict and austere military rulers. It was pragmatic, its teaching methods were direct, and because it had come from

A Zen monk practicing za-zen meditation, which was promoted by Dogen.

China, it had a cultural antecedence which the new, indigenous sects lacked. The warrior-regents of the Hojo family, who succeeded the Minamoto Shoguns in 1203, became devoted patrons of Zen. In 1247 Hojo Tokiyori (1246–56) received the Boddhisattva precepts from Dogen, who was ordered to make the long journey from Eiheiji to teach in Kamakura. However, Dogen was not prepared to stay permanently in the military capital, and it was Rinzai Zen which came to dominate the religious life of Kamakura.

In 1246 a Chinese Rinzai master, named Tao Lung (1203–1278) arrived in Japan at the invitation of a group of Japanese monks who had met him during a pilgrimage to China. Tokiyori invited him to Kamakura and in 1253 built the temple of Kenchoji and installed Tao Lung as the first teacher there.

Tao Lung transmitted the Dharma to many of his students in Kamakura, in spite of the fact that he spoke very little Japanese and few of his samurai hosts could understand Chinese. Interviews between teacher and student at Kenchoji were conducted through interpreters and by necessity relied on few words. Tao Lung's followers were largely unfamiliar with the classical koan collections of ancestral Zen, and he was not in a position to change that. So teaching instead developed around the individual needs of students and every day events in the capital became the subject of Shikin—on-the-instant—koan. These changes gave Kamakura Zen especial relevance to its adherents, and because most of them were from samurai families, the new style of practice has been labeled "warrior Zen."

There was a peculiar urgency about the practice of early warrior Zen that made it particularly effective as a teaching method. The supremacy of the Shogunate had been forged by war, and had to be maintained by constant military vigilance against disloyalty within the state and, during the thirteenth century, against the ever present threat of invasion by the Mongol hoards of mainland Asia. In these circumstances, Tao Lung and his associates found that, in so far as warriors aspired to practice Zen at all, they did so with a deadly earnest that is not encountered in times of peace and prosperity. The warriors lived in the constant knowledge that they might be called upon to lay down their lives at any time. Attachment to hearth and home or wealth and privilege were not serious distractions to them. They needed a practice in which they could find immediate peace of mind and fearlessness in the face of battle. A number of warriors became Nyudo, lay monks, who shaved their heads and took the precepts, but still lived with their families and trained for war.

Many women of samurai descent studied Zen too. Some became ordained nuns and completed the Rinzai training. One prominent example was the nun Shido, the widow of the military ruler Hojo Tokimune (ruled 1268–84); she founded the training convent of Tokeiji in 1285. In 1304 she received the transmission of the Dharma from Chokei, fourth teacher at Kenchoji.

It is recorded that the Hojo military rulers Tokiyori and Tokimune were both committed Zen students guided by Tao Lung, and later, master Tsu Yuen (1226–1286), who arrived from China in 1280 at Tokimune's invitation.

Tokimune built the temple of Enkakuji and, having installed Tsu Yuen as the first abbot, consulted him regularly throughout the turbulent years of his rule. On Tokimune's death at the age of 33, Tsu Yuen pronounced him a Boddhisattva who had ruled for 20 years without showing joy or anger— having successfully repulsed two attempted invasions by the Mongols, he showed no elation. According to Tsu Yuen, Tokimune had attained mastery of the Way.

The on-the-instant koan were cataloged into a record of Kamakura Zen, the *Shonankattoroku*, which did not fall into disuse until about 300 years later. These koan provide a fascinating glimpse of the creativity and vitality of Zen training during the 13th and 14th centuries in Japan. By way of example, one of the koan records the circumstances in which master Chokei gave the nun Shido the inka (Dharma transmission). The head monk at Enkakuji doubted Chokei's judgment about Shido's spiritual attainment and wanted to test her. He pointed out that it was traditional for one who received inka to take the high seat of the teacher and discourse on the *Rinzairoku*. This record of the Rinzai lineage would have been written in Chinese, and senior monks would have been expected to have read and studied it thoroughly. Could Shido, the head monk demanded, really brandish the staff of the Dharma from the teacher's seat? Could she speak on the *Rinzairoku* with authority and insight? It is possible that Shido had not, and indeed could not, read that text, in which case the challenge was a serious attempt to undermine her. However, Chokei's assessment of Shido's realization was sound, and she gave as good as she got. Drawing from her waist band the knife carried by all women of the samurai class, she raised it overhead and declared:

No doubt a Zen priest of the lineage of the ancestors should take the high seat and teach from ancient texts. I, however, am a woman of warrior descent and declare the Dharma face to face with sword drawn! What use have I for ancient texts?

The samurai followers of Rinzai practiced Zen by embracing their lives in the situations in which they found themselves. They did not try to make

A Japanese Zen Buddhist priest strikes the bowl-shaped gong of bronze that summons to prayer and meditation.

themselves conform to any preconception of what Zen practice was like on the Asian mainland.

Life at Eiheiji in remote Echizen province was rather different. There, Dogen insisted the monks follow the austere regime he had seen at Master Rujing's monastery in China. This fact, coupled with the distance from the capital, meant that the numbers of trainees were relatively few. After the death of Ejo in 1280, they began to drift away and for a time there was a question mark over the school's survival. Thanks, however, to the work of Keizan Jokin (1264–1325) the Soto sect not only survived but also grew to be the second largest Japanese Buddhist organization. Eiheiji remained a center for secluded meditation, but in 1321 Keizan founded a second principal temple called Sojiji and gave Soto teachings to the masses. His importance to the Soto lineage can be assessed from his posthumous title "Taiso," meaning great patriarch, which is comparable only with that given to Dogen himself: "Koso," the eminent patriarch. Counted amongst Keizan's achievements is the *Denkoroku*, a literary record of the genealogy of the Soto teachers traced from Ejo back to Shakyamuni Buddha. This work tends to be regarded almost as highly as Dogen's *Shobogenzo* in the Soto School. Keizan's successor as abbot of Sojiji, Gasan Joseki

(1275–1365), had very many disciples, and the spread of Soto throughout Japan is attributed to twenty-five of them.

The major influence in the Rinzai School during these formative years came from the Otokan Lineage. The name Otokan is an amalgamation of the names of three masters: O of Dio Kokushi or Nanpo Jomyo (1235–1308), TO of Daito Kokushi or Shuho Myochu (1282–1337) and KAN of Kanzan Egan Kokushi (1277–1360).

Dio brought this branch of Rinzai Zen from China and did much to enable it to take root in Japan. Daito was the first master in this lineage who didn't wish to travel to China for his studies. After his enlightenment he practiced in relative seclusion for at least ten years, some of that time practicing among the beggars. His fame spread and he came to the attention of the Emperor who, hearing that he liked melons, sent a messenger out with instructions to offer a melon to the beggars on the the condition that "they receive it without using their hands". The messenger found Daito when he replied "I will take it if you give it to me without using hands." He was caught by his own wisdom.

Two emperors supported Daito and one, Hanazono, became a serious student of Zen. Through this support, Daito was able to establish Daitokuji temples in Kyoto and Myoshinji. His effect on Japanese Rinzai Zen is profound, especially in the establishment of a capping phrase system used in conjunction with koan study. His final admonitions are still chanted in Rinzai monasteries today.

Kanzan Kokushi inherited Myoshinji temple as one of the major training monasteries in Japan, and also inherited the emperor Hanazono as a student. Kanzan practiced deeply and sincerely and although it is said that he never lectured, the effects of his practice are felt today in the Rinzai school.

If Soto established itself as an independent school by Dogen's insistence on secluded zazen and his open criticism of the old orthodoxies, the Rinzai sect owes it independent foundation as the dominant Zen school of this time to the achievements of the immigrant Chinese Ch'an masters and indigenous Japanese masters, in close association with the military overlords of Kamakura. The partnership forged through this association left Zen shot through, as it were, with a martial tone, which it has never entirely shaken off.

Nevertheless, Zen flourished under Hojo rule. Other Chinese teachers arrived, fleeing the Mongol armies sweeping across Asia, and as many as 27 separate Rinzai lineages established themselves around the capital.

In 1338 the political leadership of the nation passed from the Hojo to the Ashikaga family, which provided the occupants of the office of Shogun until 1573. In this, the Muromachi era, the seat of government returned to the re-named city of Kyoto. Japanese Buddhism, dominated now by Rinzai Zen, entered its golden age. The ten main Zen temples of Kyoto and Kamakura were ranked and re-organized on a Chinese social model called Gozan, the five mountains, under the auspices of Nanzenji in Kyoto. Zen found its ceremonial role in the life of the capital and was embraced by the Emperors, the Shogunate, the aristocracy, and commoners alike. There was a flowering of higher education and Zen-inspired arts and crafts, including landscape gardening, poetry, calligraphy, and painting.

In the end, however, institutionalism set in, the arts became ever more profane, and the creativity and spontaneity of the Zen training available in the Gozan temples began to deteriorate. A famous and popular Zen monk of the later Muromachi era, Ikkyu Sojun (1394–1481), said that the temples had all lost their transmission, and as if to prove the point, tore up his own inka certificate. He had studied at Daitokuji, a temple outside the Gozan system, which did manage to retain a vibrant core of Zen practice. In general though, the fate of Rinzai Zen during the Muromachi era was too closely linked to the fortunes of the Ashikaga Shoguns, whose lives of increasing indolence and opulence belied the rising threat to their power from more provincial warlords and some very disaffected sections of the lower classes.

Japan's middle ages were brought to a close by nearly two hundred years of civil war, ending finally at the battle of Sekigahara in 1600, after which the victorious Tokugawa Ieyasu (1542–1616) founded the third and final Shogunate and moved the capital to Edo (modern Tokyo).

Ieyasu's reign heralded an era of lasting peace and a revival of authentic Zen practice. The cultural and intellectual Zen of the Gozan system was rejected in favor of a reinvestigation of the Chinese Zen records and the re-discovery of many long forgotten teachings. At the same time, there was a move away from the discredited and corrupted monastic hierarchies, and an active search for a more spiritually motivated form of practice. Pilgrimage and travel were safe once more, and a new sect of Zen appeared from China. Known as Obaku, it was established at Mapukuji near Kyoto in 1661 by the Chinese master Yin-Yuan Lungi-chi (1592–1673). The Obaku sect combined Zen with Sutra study and the doctrines of Pure Land Buddhism. The school survives, but it has never had the popularity of Rinzai and Soto.

One of the Zen teachers of the early Edo era was Takuan Soho (1573–1645), the founding abbot of Takaiji in1638 and a renowned artist, calligrapher, and master of the tea ceremony. He is perhaps best known as a friend and mentor to the Shogun Iemitsu (ruled 1623–1651), the Yagyu Shinkage Ryu sword master Yagyu Munenori (1571–1646), and the so-called sword saint Miyamoto Musashi (1584–1645). It is really down to Takuan's efforts that an association emerged between the art of the Japanese sword and Zen. During the Kamakura era, Zen masters had drawn analogies from the lives of warriors to illustrate spiritual truths. Takuan went a stage further and

encouraged warriors to keep studying the martial arts in peacetime on the basis that the single-minded study of swordsmanship can induce a spiritual awakening similar to that attained by za-zen. In so teaching, he laid the philosophical foundations upon which purely military martial arts (Bujutsu) were able to evolve into practices for self-discipline, character development, and eventually, sport (Budo).

Another important teacher of this era was Bankei Yotaku (1622–1693) whose clarity of spiritual insight and easy-going teaching style attracted many admirers. He promoted no particular practice, and taught in a way that seems surprisingly modern. The unborn Buddha Mind functions freely and constantly in everyone, he said. Therefore the realization of this truth is as accessible in walking and working as it is in meditation. He saw no need for any special situation, dogma, method, or teacher in order to realize the "unborn."

The reforms made by Hakuin Ekaku (1686–1768) are the source of much of what is today recognized as Rinzai Zen. Hakuin is one of the most important figures in the history of Japanese Zen. He underwent a profound enlightenment experience and went on to guide many students through the strict training methods inherited from Tang and Sung China. In addition, his extensive social works among the poor made him a popular figure of folklore. His success as a reformer lay in bringing together the many disparate strands of Rinzai training and systematizing them in a way that was at once innovative but quite orthodox. Koan study was central to his method, and he brought the ancient Chinese collections together into an ordered sequence with many of more modern inspiration. Hakuin's Dharma grandchildren, Inzan and Takuju, whose lineages form the main two Rinzai lines of today, completed this systemization. The famous koan about the sound of one hand clapping is attributed to Hakuin, as are many of the characteristics of modern Zen training: intensive meditation retreats (sesshin), Dharma talks (teisho), and private interviews with the teacher (dokusan or sanzen).

The Soto sect also went through a period of rejuvenation during the mid-Edo period, with the Zen masters Menzan Zuiho (1683–1769) and Tenkei Denson (1648–1735) being the main reformers. Menzan encouraged a return to a more fundamental approach and emphasized Dogen's "Just sitting and dropping off body and mind." Tenkei's approach included the Rinzai School's use of koan study and he developed a radical interpretation of Dogen's *Shobogenzo*. Between them, they gave the flagging Soto school fresh impetus.

Apart from its impact on swordsmanship, the influence of the Zen of the Edo era may be seen in the well-loved poetry of the layman Bassho (1644–1694) and the monk Ryokan (1758–1831). However, it did not play the dominant cultural role it had enjoyed in the Muromachi era. Like all the Buddhist schools, its influence and creativity were stultified by edict of the Shogunate which, in the mid-eighteenth century, required every religious sect to catalog and register all its dogmas and teachings. All teachers had to submit to the authority of central monasteries, in turn controlled by the military government, and laymen were not allowed to teach, even if they had received Dharma transmission. Innovation was forbidden!

The situation did not immediately improve after the Shogunate was overthrown in 1868 and replaced by direct Imperial rule. For some time during the Meiji era (1868–1912) the new government attacked Zen as a foreign religion associated with the nation's feudal past. A new form of state Shinto based on the divinity of the Emperor led to the conversion of many Buddhist temples into Shinto shrines. The situation was further complicated by the opening up of Japan to trade with the international community after nearly 400 years of isolation imposed by the Tokugawa Shoguns. In the drive towards modernization and reform, many people associated Western technology with Western religious beliefs, and proselytizing Christian missionaries maximized on the opportunity to criticize Buddhism.

It was clear that monastic Buddhism, including Zen, was moribund. To guarantee the survival of their schools and meet the criticism leveled at them, teachers began to re-examine the Sutras and other texts from which their dogmas, practices, and temples had emerged. Some found fresh impetus by retrenching in tradition or secluded practice, others concentrated their efforts on promoting the benefits of za-zen or the martial arts, and others met their critics by academic argument based on Western models.

A leading light in the initiative to promote zazen outside the temples was Nantembo (1839–1925), who abandoned his support for monastic training altogether and concentrated on leading intensive Zen retreats, free from ceremony and dogma, for the new ruling classes.

The Zen teachers who came to prominence during the Meiji era were those with an open-minded and forward-looking outlook, who were prepared to re-evaluate the relevance of their inherited training methods for people living outside the confines of a monastic cloister. An outstanding example was Shaku Soen (1856–1919), who was able to explain Buddhism in rational and scientific terms and traveled widely. In 1893 he spoke at the World Parliament of Religions in Chicago, which marked the beginning of serious Western interest in the practice of eastern religions, as opposed to the mere academic study of them. It was Shaku Soen's student Suzuki Daisetz Teitaro (1870–1966) who was then to publish so much about the rich heritage of Zen and begin the process of making it accessible in the West.

A modern-day Zen monk sits on the verandha overlooking the raked sand garden, part of the Great Sea Garden, Daisen-in temple, Kyoto.

The Ox-Herding Pictures

The path of Zen has been written about in many different ways, but one of the most helpful for understanding its essence is through the pictorial representation of the parable of the Ox-herding pictures. These illustrations have been used to illuminate Zen teachings ever since they were first produced during the Sung dynasty in China. There are four well-known versions of them, along with associated interpretations, commentaries, and poems. The best known stem from the Chinese Ch'an (Zen) master K'uo-an Chih-yuan (Jap., Kakuan Shien), who belonged to the Rinzai school. The ox-herding drawings tell the story of the stages passed through by a Zen practitioner as he searches for, finds, and then lives according to his true nature. In the pictures, the ox represents Buddha-nature or one's true self, and the ox-herd, the human being. In the beginning of the series, the ox and the ox-herd are two separate entities, but as the story progresses they gradually become one. The ox was one of the most common of domestic animals in China at the time these drawings were made and it is interesting to note how characteristic it is of Ch'an to take such a practical animal for its representation of Buddha nature.

Kakuan's pictures are best known via copies made by the famous Japanese Zen painter Shunbun (died about 1460), one of the greatest painters in black and white of the Ashikaga period (1333–1573). The original Shunbun ox-herd paintings are preserved at Shokokuji Temple, Kyoto. The series unfolds as follows:

1)   The ox-herd has lost his ox; he feels rootless and homeless.
2)   Despite his confusion, he searches and finds traces of the ox.
3)   He follows the tracks and finds the ox, but still does not have any sense of how to control it.
4)   With great effort, he attempts to tame the ox, but it is a difficult and tough struggle. He has to be hard on the ox.
5)   He succeeds and is able to set the ox out to pasture, but only under close surveillance.
6)   The struggle is over: he is on the ox's back and is able to ride home relaxed enough to play the flute. The joy of the ox-herd intimates he has achieved freedom from the world of appearances, of gain and loss.

7)   The ox-herd is alone. He no longer sees the ox as separate from himself or needs it as a symbol or concept. In the absence of these distinctions, he can be in solitude and serenity.

8)   Both the ox-herd and the ox have disappeared. All illusions have been dropped; even the idea of holiness has vanished, and in this state of emptiness the fullness of life is experienced.

9)   Out of this formless awareness, form is embodied and observed just as it is, endlessly changing. Rivers flow, birds fly, trees blossom.

10) The ox-herd returns to town. Oneness and twoness have been transcended. He is a free man, being fully himself, with nothing to gain or lose. He manifests enlightenment and, true to the Bodhisattva ideal, forgoes personal liberation to help others.

Several other versions of the ox-herding pictures have also been drawn. Here we present the woodcut prints of Tomikichiro Tokuriti, accompanied by the poem and commentary by Kakuan for each stage of the original Ox-herding pictures:

ONE

The beast has never gone astray, and what is the use of searching for him? The reason why the ox-herd is not on intimate terms with him is because the ox-herd himself has violated his own inmost nature. The beast is lost, for the ox-herd has himself been led out of the way through his deluding senses. His home is receding farther away from him, and byways and crossways are ever confused. Desire for gain and fear of loss burn like fires; ideas of right and wrong shoot up like a phalanx.

Alone in the wilderness, lost in the jungle,
     the boy is searching, searching!
The swelling waters, the far-away mountains,
     and the unending path;
Exhausted and in despair, he knows not where to go,
He only hears the evening cicadas singing in the maple-woods.

TWO

By the aid of the sutras and by inquiring into the doctrines, he has come to understand something, he has found the traces. He now knows that vessels, however varied, are all of gold, and that the objective world is a reflection of the Self. Yet, he is unable to distinguish what is good from what is not; his mind is still confused as to the truth and falsehood. As he has not yet entered the gate, he is provisionally said to have noticed the traces.

By the stream and under the trees, scattered are the
    traces of the lost;
The sweet-scented grasses are growing thick—did he
    find the way?
However remote over the hills and far away the beast
    may wander,
His nose reaches the heavens and none can conceal it.

THREE

The boy finds the way by the sound he hears; he sees thereby into the origin of things, and all his senses are in harmonious order. In all his activities, it is manifestly present. It is like the salt in water and the glue in color. (It is there, though not distinguishable as an individual entity.) When the eye is properly directed, he will find that it is no other than himself.

On a yonder branch perches a nightingale cheerfully
  singing;
The sun is warm, and a soothing breeze blows, on the bank
  the willows are green;
The ox is there all by himself, nowhere is he to hide
  himself;
The splendid head decorated with stately horns—what
  painter can reproduce him?

FOUR

Lost long in the wilderness, the boy has at last found the ox and his hands are on him. But, owing to the overwhelming pressure of the outside world, the ox is hard to keep under control. He constantly longs for the old sweet-scented field. The wild nature is still unruly, and altogether refuses to be broken. If the ox-herd wishes to see the ox completely in harmony with himself, he is surely to use the whip freely.

With the energy of his whole being, the boy has at last
    taken hold of the ox;
But how wild his will, how ungovernable his power!
At times he struts up a plateau,
When lo! he is lost again in a misty unpenetrable
    mountain-pass.

FIVE

When a thought moves, another follows, and then another—an endless train of thoughts is thus awakened. Through enlightenment, all this turns into truth; but falsehood asserts itself when confusion prevails. Things oppress us not because of an objective world, but because of a self-deceiving mind. Do not let the nose-string loose, hold it tight, and allow no vacillation.

The boy is not to separate himself with his whip and tether,
Lest the animal should wander away into a world
of defilements;
When he is properly tended to, he will grow pure
and docile;
Without a chain, nothing binding, he will by himself
follow the ox-herd.

SIX

The struggle is over; gain and loss, the man is no more concerned with. He hums a rustic tune of the woodsman, he sings simple songs of the village-boy. Saddling himself on the ox's back, his eyes are fixed at things not of the earth, earthly. Even if he is called, he will not turn his head; however enticed, he will no more be kept back.

Riding on the animal, he leisurely wends his way home;
Enveloped in the evening mist, how tunefully the flute
     vanishes away!
Singing a ditty, beating time, his heart is filled with a joy
     indescribable!
That he is now one of those who know, need it be told?

SEVEN

The Dharmas are one and the ox is symbolic. When you know that what you need is not the snare or set-net but the hare or fish; it is like gold separated from the dross, it is like the moon rising out of the clouds. The one ray of light, serene and penetrating, shines even before days of creation.

Riding on the animal, he is at last back in his home,
Where lo! the ox is no more; the man alone sits serenely.
Though the red sun is high up in the sky, he is still quietly
*   dreaming,*
Under a straw-thatched roof are his whip and rope
*   idly lying.*

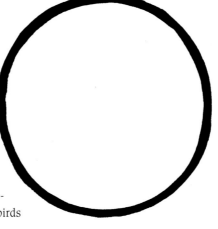

EIGHT

All confusion is set aside, and serenity alone prevails; even the idea of holiness does not obtain. He does not linger about where the Buddha is; and where there is no Buddha, he speedily passes by. When there exists no form of dualism, even a thousand-eyed one fails to detect a loophole. A holiness before which birds offer flowers is but a farce.

All is empty—the whip, the rope, the man, and the ox;
Who can ever survey the vastness of heaven?
Over the furnace burning ablaze, not a flake of snow can fall:
When this state of things obtains, manifest is the spirit of
the ancient master.

NINE

From the very beginning, pure and immaculate, the man has never been affected by defilement. He watches the growth of things, while himself abiding in the immovable serenity of non-assertion. He does not identify himself with the māyā-like transformations (that are going on about him), nor has he any use of himself (which is artificiality). The waters are blue, the mountains are green; sitting alone, he observes things undergoing changes.

To return to the Origin, to be back at the Source—already a false step this!
Far better it is to stay home, blind and deaf, and without much ado;
Sitting in the hut, he takes no cognizance of things outside,
Behold the streams flowing—whither nobody knows; and the flowers vividly red—for whom are they?

TEN

His thatched cottage gate is closed, and even the wisest know him not. No glimpses of his inner life are to be caught; for he goes on his own way without following the steps of the ancient sages. Carrying a gourd, he goes out into the market; leaning against a staff, he comes home. He is found in company with wine-bibbers and butchers; he and they are all converted into Buddhas.

*Bare-chested and bare-footed, he comes out into
    the market-place;
Daubed with mud and ashes, how broadly he smiles!
There is no need for the miraculous power of the gods,
For he touches, and lo! the dead trees are in full bloom.*

Kakuan's ox-herding pictures were the most popular series in Japan, but at about the time of their first publication another set of ten drawings was in vogue in China. They were introduced in 1585 with drawings by an unknown artist and poems by Pu-ming, himself unknown except for his name. The Five Pictures of Ching-chu (in Japanese, Seikyo) and the Six Pictures of Tzu-te, (in Japanese, Jitoku) inspired them. Seikyo and Jitoku were Chinese Ch-an (Zen) masters of about the 12th century. The symbolism used in their pictures, which differentiates them from Kakuan's, was based on the changing color of the ox from dark to light.

The contemporary Zen master Shibayama Zenkei made a series of ten drawings by the unknown artist available to the West. In his pictures, the ox is initially a dark color, which signifies ignorance and delusion. The color gradually whitens, and the ox is simultaneously tamed; this signifies the awakening to one's true nature. According to master Shibayama, the transformation is aided by the "tether of faith" and "rod of striving" (great faith and great endurance) which goad the "ox-mind" forward. These were accompanied by Pu-ming's poems, which are as follows:

1. UNDISCIPLINED

With his horns fiercely projected in the air the beast snorts,
Madly running over the mountain paths, farther and farther
he goes astray!
A dark cloud is spread across the entrance of the valley,
And who knows how much of the fine fresh herb is trampled
under his wild hoofs!

2. DISCIPLINE BEGUN

I am in possession of a straw rope, and I pass it through his nose,
For once he makes a frantic attempt to run away, but he is
severely whipped and whipped;
The beast resists the training with all the power there is in a
nature wild and ungoverned,
But the rustic ox-herd never relaxes his pulling tether and ever-
ready whip.

3. IN HARNESS

*Gradually getting into harness the beast is now content to be
led by the nose,
Crossing the stream, walking along the mountain path, he
follows every step of the leader;
The leader holds the rope tightly in his hand never letting it go,
All day long he is on the alert, almost unconscious of what
fatigue is.*

4. FACED ROUND

*After long days of training the result begins to tell and the beast
is faced round,
A nature so wild and ungoverned is finally broken, he has become
gentler;
But the tender has not yet given him his full confidence,
He still keeps his straw rope with which the ox is now tied to a
tree.*

5. TAMED

*Under the green willow tree and by the ancient mountain
stream,
The ox is set at liberty to pursue his own pleasures;
At the eventide when a gray mist descends on the
pasture,
The boy wends his homeward way with the animal
quietly following.*

6. UNIMPEDED

*On the verdant field the beast contentedly lies idling his
    time away,
No whip is needed now, nor any kind of restraint;
The boy too sits leisurely under the pine tree,
Playing a tune of peace, overflowing with joy.*

7. LAISSEZ-FAIRE

*The spring stream in the evening sun flows languidly
    along the willow-lined bank,
In the hazy atmosphere the meadow grass is seen
    growing thick;
When hungry he grazes, when thirsty he quaffs, as time
    sweetly slides,
While the boy on the rock dozes for hours not noticing
    anything that goes on about him.*

8. ALL FORGOTTEN

*The beast all in white now is surrounded by the white
    clouds,
The man is perfectly at his ease and carefree,
    so is his companion;
The white clouds penetrated by the moonlight cast their
    white shadows below,
The white clouds and the bright moonlight—each
    following its course of movement.*

9. THE SOLITARY MOON

Nowhere is the beast, and the oxherd is master of his time,
He is a solitary cloud wafting lightly along the mountain peaks;
Clapping his hands he sings joyfully in the moonlight,
But remember a last wall is still left barring his homeward walk.

10. BOTH VANISHED

Both the man and the animal have disappeared, no traces are left,
The bright moonlight is empty and shadowless with all the ten
thousand objects in it;
If anyone should ask the meaning of this,
Behold the lilies of the field and its fresh sweet-scented verdure.

Zen Practice in Daily Life

PART 1

The first part of this chapter is devoted to the practice of za-zen meditation, the second to the spiritual dilemmas, practical problems, and other questions that arise out of our practice.

Here is a pane of frosted glass and we are living on this side, which is called the dualistic world, and behind the glass there is a world which might be called the monistic world, the world of oneness. Since we are living in this dualistic world there is a lot of confusion, but as a result of our concentration, as a result of our Zazen, we are able to attain satori experience, even though shallow. Now this shallow experience may be compared with a very tiny spot on this frosted glass, which becomes transparent. We are able to see through this small spot into oneness; we may be very much surprised at what we see, but we are no longer cheated by duality. But if we do not continue our Zazen, even though we see oneness through the one small spot, the glass will become frosted over again, and only the memory remains. That memory is still alive within us, but now it is only a memory—no longer a fact.

Constant practice of zazen will enlarge that transparent spot in the frosted glass. The more we do zazen, the larger the spot becomes. Buddha's enlightenment is a complete circle, but ours at present only the size of a fingernail.

From a talk by Hakuun Yasutani Roshi

In a general sense, the Rinzai schools of Zen place emphasis on koan study as a practice toward enlightenment, while the Soto schools concentrate on practice as enlightenment and may not use any koan work in their training. There are some schools that make use of the teaching methods of both the Soto and Rinzai traditions and the teacher may choose to ask a student to emphasize a particular practice, depending on what is personally appropriate. However, in all schools of Zen the real core of the practice is za-zen (or seated meditation).

In our daily lives, za-zen provides us with a situation in which we can remove ourselves from external activities, turn our attention inward, and face ourselves. Za-zen is not about achieving some particular state of consciousness. Rather, it is about discovering who you are and what your life is. In za-zen, once we have sat and assumed our best posture, we sit in silence. If our practice is counting breaths (see p. 108), we begin to count breaths. People sitting for the first time in their lives become astonished at how the constant activity of their minds interrupts what initially seemed the simple task of focusing on the breath. This mind activity is normal and is a phenomenon initially experienced by all. However, the mind and the body are interdependent and we discover that za-zen in the correct posture encourages this flow of thoughts to slow down. With practice, we discover we can move from being "lost" in our thoughts to being conscious of them. At this stage we observe them and then let them go, each time coming back to the breath.

As thoughts arise, we try not to censor or repress them. Nothing is taboo. Whatever arises may be observed without judgement and then allowed to pass like clouds in the sky. Some difficult issues will nevertheless keep arising. In this case, you may decide to let your thoughts run their course and experience, on the cushion, the emotions they arouse in you. With experience you will become more confident of facing, accepting, and then releasing these painful inner conflicts, each time returning to the breath. Over time, inner tensions are eased, the mind begins to settle down, and inner spaciousness arises.

It is worth noting that the process of za-zen is not limited. It is an unending, ceaseless activity of self-realization, identical for people with long experience of the practice and those new to it. Master Dogen said in his treatise *Shobogenzo*: "Za-zen by a beginner is also the whole experience of the fundamental truth." Another Zen teacher said: "When we do za-zen, we sit immediately in the same condition of body and mind as Gautama Buddha, and in this sense there is no difference between men of experience and beginners in this condition." And Dogen once again: "... there is no question here at all of being intelligent or stupid, nor is there any difference between the quick-witted and the dull. If you exert yourself single-mindedly [in za-zen], this is practicing the Way itself. Practice and realization leave not a trace of impurity, and the person who advances in the Way is an ordinary person."

Where and When to Sit

A great advantage of za-zen is that it does not require much space to practice, although ideally where you choose should be quiet and unlikely to be disturbed. Keep the area clean and, if possible, reserve it only for your za-zen practice. You may wish to install a small altar on which to place a statue of the Buddha or other inspirational figure, an incense holder, and perhaps a tiny vase for flowers, although none of these things is in any way essential. The temperature should be comfortable—that is, warm in the winter and cool in the summer. The lighting should be normal, neither too dark nor too light. Natural lighting, when available, is the best. The essential idea is to maintain continuity so that whenever you enter the area set aside for za-zen, the setting and the smell (if you use incense) are the same. In this way, you will begin to associate za-zen practice with these surroundings and you will be able to settle down more quickly.

It is best to practice za-zen at a regular time or times every day. Early morning, noon, early evening, and before going to bed are the best times. If you can find time for only one session, a morning sitting is the one to choose. If you wish to sit twice a day, the morning and before bedtime sittings are the best. To begin with, 15–20 minutes is enough. Build up to 30 minutes–1hour, depending on your particular situation.

The Postures

There are a number of postures that can be used. You should try each of them to discover which suits you best. Persevere with one of the more stable postures even if it seems uncomfortable at first. Patience and practice are needed for good posture.

The recommended postures are described here in increasing order of their stability, balance, and conduciveness to good practice. It is perfectly acceptable to start with posture 1 and very few people can sit in posture 5. In all postures, the ideal is to sit in such a way that the body is perfectly upright, so that a vertical line can be drawn from the center of your forehead, nose, chin, throat, and navel. This is achieved by pushing the waist forward and the abdomen out. In this position the weight of the body is focused on the belly or lower abdomen. This area is the focus of za-zen breathing and concentration. The eyes are half-open and focused on the ground about 3–6 feet (1–2 meters) in front of you. In some schools of Zen, it is also permitted to keep the eyes closed (as long as you do not doze off!).

Posture 1

This posture is for people who are very stiff through lack of exercise or because of age. Sit facing a blank wall on a stool or chair that is of a height

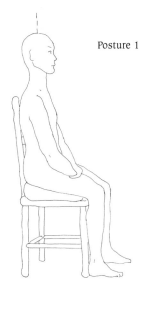

Posture 1

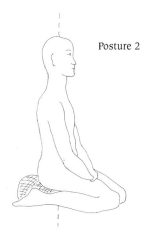

Posture 2

that lets you set your feet firmly on the ground. If you are tall, adjust your height with a firm cushion on the seat or, if small, a thick plank of wood on the floor beneath your feet. Set your back straight, shoulders down and head held upright, not stiff, more as though a thin line of cotton runs from your head to the ceiling. Rest your hands on your lap, right hand under left hand, palms turned upward. The thumbs touch at the tips and form a parallel line with your fingers.

For the next four positions, you need a folded blanket about 3 feet (1 meter) square and a firm cushion. Set the cushion on the blanket; the postures are taken up with the cushion under your bottom.

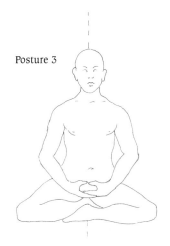

Posture 3

Posture 2

This is the easiest position for beginners. Straddle the mat so that you are sitting on your knees, shins and insteps, and bottom. A triangle is formed by your knees and bottom. Head, shoulder, and hands are the same as in position 1.

Posture 3

This is the Burmese position, a posture most popular with Western followers of Zen. The legs are crossed, but both feet are flat on the blanket. The bottom is situated on the first third to a half of the cushion. Both knees should be touching the blanket.

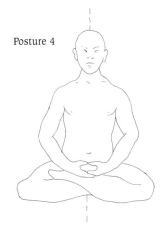

Posture 4

If they are not, you may help get them down by putting a second cushion under your bottom, or you can place a small cushion under the knee or knees that stick up. It is important to be sitting on a firm base, formed by the triangle of your knees and bottom. Head, shoulders, and hands are the same as in position 1.

Posture 4

This is the half-lotus position. The left foot is under the right thigh and the right foot is on the left thigh, or vice versa. Both variations are equally good. This posture is quite difficult for the beginner.

Posture 5

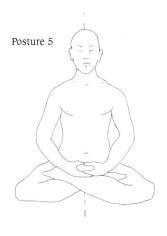

Posture 5

This is the full lotus position, in which the right foot rests on the left thigh and the left foot rests on the right thigh. The lotus is the best and strongest sitting position since it forms a perfect triangle between the knees and bottom and produces great stability. Unfortunately, the lotus is also the most difficult posture to achieve and usually out of reach of the beginner and even many mature students. Do not worry if you cannot do a lotus—most of us can't either!

Za-zen Checklist

1. Sit on the forward half of your zafu (the black round cushion).
2. Arrange your legs—full lotus, half lotus, Burmese, kneeling, or chair; choose the position you can sustain most comfortably and with stability.
3. Center your spine by swaying in decreasing arcs.
4. Straighten and extend your spine and align your head (by "pushing up to the ceiling" and then relaxing). Origin of thrust is at base of spine. Belly and buttocks both protrude slightly.
5. Head—should not tilt forward or lean to either side.
    Ears—should be parallel with shoulders.
    Tip of nose—centered over navel.
    Chin—tucked in slightly.
6. Eyes—neither fully opened nor fully closed, lowered to 45° angle; unfocused, "gazing" at direction of floor 3–4 feet (about 1 meter) in front. If you are closer than that to a wall, then "look through it," at where the floor would be. Thus, blinking is minimized.
7. Mouth—lips and teeth closed; place the tip of the tongue against the roof of the mouth, just behind the front teeth. Swallow any saliva in your mouth, and evacuate the air so there is a slight vacuum. This inhibits salivation.
8. Hands—"cosmic" mudra:
    right—palm up, "blade" against lower belly.
    left—on top of right, middle knuckles overlap.
    thumb—tips lightly touch, forming an oval.
9. Make sure your whole body is arranged the way you want it before beginning za-zen.
10. Keep as still as possible during za-zen.
11. When you finish za-zen, remain quiet and calm initially and move only slowly out of the posture.

Counting Breaths

After getting into a good posture, practice focusing your attention by counting breaths. To begin with, you can count the "in"-breaths and the "out"-breaths. Thus, as you inhale, count *one*; as you exhale, count *two*. The count should be inaudible. Do not try to control the breath. Let it be as it is. Just encourage it, even if it feels tense and shallow. As you are counting, you will inevitably have some thought or other. As soon as you notice you have stopped counting breaths, begin again at *one*. If you can reach *ten* without an interfering thought, go back to *one* and start again. Do the same if you find you have counted beyond *ten*. Do not be surprised if it takes a lot of practice before you can concentrate only on your breath. After some practice, you could start counting only "out"-breaths.

For most of us, many weeks, months, or years will pass by before we can truly, consistently count to ten without a distracting thought. This is quite natural since what we are doing is developing our ability just to be completely present in the moment. For most of us, the feeling of having nothing to do is uncomfortable, and, as we have discussed, our minds will try to fill the gap with an amazing variety of thoughts. Gradually, we learn to sit for longer and longer periods.

Do not see this practice of counting breaths as something that is easy or as one that you wish to move on from quickly. Sitting in za-zen and counting breaths is a complete practice and one that deserves our full attention if we are not to waste our time on the cushion.

Clothes and Equipment

Loose clothing is essential to let you sit and breathe freely. Dark clothing, black preferably, is recommended, particularly if you sit with a Zen group. Bright colors may distract the concentration of others. Whatever clothes you wear, they should be clean and fresh.

You will need a firm cushion which should be placed on a flat blanket if the floor is hard or, if not, directly on the carpet. In Zen monasteries and Zen sitting groups, monks and lay people usually sit on a small, black, round cushion called a *zafu* which is placed on a black mat called a *zabuton* (about 3 feet/1 meter square). Zafus are approximately 15 inches (38 centimeters) in diameter and 2–4 inches (5–10 centimeters) thick. They are normally packed tight with kapok. Some people use two zafus or make one higher by placing another cushion or a folded blanket underneath it.

The advice on za-zen posture and equipment is quoted from *The Elements of Zen* (see p. 192).

Koan Practice

The koan system is the unique and traditional teaching method of the Rinzai School of Zen Buddhism. The koans derive from actual encounters, usually (but not always) between accomplished Zen masters and their students. Successive generations of teachers have related these encounters to their students to illustrate particular principles of Zen. Questions or problems, often paradoxical, highlighted by each story were presented to students to encourage and test them in their own training. Over time, the encounters and their associated problems were formalized and systematized into koan collections like the *Mumonkan*, the *Hekiganroku*, the *Tetteki Tosui*, and the *Shoyoroku*.

The koan system enables the Zen teacher to test the individual student's understanding of Zen, not intellectually, but as it applies to the student's own life. Acting as a focus or catalyst for the student, it will confront him or her with a challenge, the resolution of which will become of tremendous personal importance and will clarify the student's understanding of Zen. Hakuin (1686–1769) said:

> If you take up one koan and investigate it without ceasing, your thoughts will die and your ego-demands will be destroyed. It is as though a vast abyss opened up in front of you, with no place to put your hands and feet. You face death, and your heart feels as though it were fire. Then suddenly you are one with the koan, and body and mind let go... This is known as seeing into one's own nature. You must push forward relentlessly, and with the help of this great concentration you will penetrate without fail to the infinite source of your own nature.

Viewed in mechanical terms, the realization arising from the resolution of a koan varies from a glimpse of the true Self (like the fractional exposure to light possible through a camera shutter) to Dai Kensho (great enlightenment) itself. But this is very provisional. It is usual for realization through koan study to mature over time, and whether the teacher sets the student to work on many koan or only one, none can be fathomed exhaustively. In fact, any experience in koan study that is regarded as an "attainment," or in some way final, usually becomes merely a memory through which the discriminating mind will judge and assess all present and future experience. The realization then becomes a lifeless burden, preventing the student from investigating each moment of the mystery of life with an open mind.

Genuine koan study is really only possible under the guidance of a teacher who has completed the same training. By the indiscriminate selection and study of koan in the absence of a teacher, the overwhelming probability is that the would-be student will settle for a very shallow, if not conceptual, resolution of it. For example, take the koan: "What was your Original Face before your parents were born?" Many people suppose they must try to imagine how they felt before they were born and embark upon all kinds of visualizations and fantasies in an attempt to recall that experience. Unless they train with a teacher, the error of this kind of approach will not become clear.

To appreciate a koan, a student must really live with it, or as Hakuin said, "become one with it." To begin with, this can feel artificial, but with determined practice in the face of repeated failure in formal interview with the teacher, the student starts to empathize with the problem the koan represents. It reveals new and different perspectives on the practice of Zen, deepening and clarifying the student's understanding in the process.

PART 2

Practice in daily life is an extension of sitting meditation. It is important to see the similarities between sitting meditation and meditation in action. In both cases, awareness continues to be present: there are bodily sensations and mental activity. In arising from the cushion, our awareness continues pretty much the same as when we are sitting. In Zen practice, sitting meditation is one part of a seamless 24-hour meditation.

The word practice implies doing something over and over again. In Zen, the practice is not to become an expert sometime in the future. It is rather to practice mindfully in this present moment, so we can appreciate what life is now. Like drinking something you enjoy, you don't worry about becoming an expert at it, you just drink it. We all know that if we are dreaming about something else, we don't enjoy the drink as much. By applying our attention here and now, we can begin to appreciate life more and living becomes more vital.

Mindfulness

If you concentrate your efforts single-mindedly, that in itself is wholeheartedly engaging the way.

Master Dogen, 1200–1253

Our first practice is mindfulness. Try to be aware of what you are doing. Notice if you have had enough of it and want to escape into a fantasy. See the fantasy, notice how much you retreat into it, and see what the cost is to you and those around you. Obviously, if you work on a machine, the results of losing awareness could be disastrous. If you are working with people, you may feel distant or even alienated through living in your own world. By bringing yourself back to this moment again and again you can begin to experience the contentment of just being, of just experiencing the

A Zen novice in gassho
(palms together) position.

momentary flow of consciousness, and the need to escape into a fantasy world will diminish. As you continue mindfulness practice, you may begin to notice the areas where communication between you and your co-workers or friends could be improved or to see where your lack of awareness can cause shoddy or unsatisfactory work. This is a difficult practice, yet if you can deal with each moment as it arises, life becomes more free, an art. You will have an opportunity to live fully, giving life to whatever you do.

An easy initial technique to apply if you are losing awareness is to slow yourself down, take a step back, take a few deep breaths, and see what is going on. By doing so, you can check on how much attention you are putting into what you are doing, and how much you are following old habits and irrelevant thinking. Through this type of practice, you can become more concentrated, less scattered, and more open to different approaches to life.

Quite often we think that our activities are pointless and hold ourselves back from being fully involved in them, thinking that we can begin to practice mindfulness when things get interesting. However, by applying ourselves to even so-called pointless tasks they become more interesting. After all, at the time they are the only life we have, the only time we have.

By applying mindfulness, we can begin to understand and appreciate life more. The mind becomes calmer, and less moved by concepts and expectations. If we are fully immersed in living each moment, there is little room for dissatisfaction.

Discrimination

Cut off the thoughts of the discriminating mind and you are no other than Buddha.

Master Rinzai Gigen (d. 866)

The discriminative function of the mind is very important to us as human beings. It enables us to make the minutest distinctions, and that function has helped us to survive until the present. Yet this function is limited; it cannot help us to determine our true nature. Good, bad, right, and wrong can never reach it, yet in our own mind we try to work out our true nature with this kind of thinking. Discrimination is, at best, a pointer; at its worst, it hinders us from fully engaging in life, ensuring that we are always standing back and evaluating how we are doing.

The way to deal with this discriminative function of the mind is to directly experience our environment, immersing ourselves in the situation and letting go of checking where we stand. Through doing so, the situation directly teaches us, revealing our nature intimately. Otherwise, what we experience is a split between what is happening and what is going on in our head, and with such a perception it is difficult to have peace in life.

Impermanence

Form and substance are like the dew on the grass, the fortune of life like the dart of lightening emptied in an instance, vanished in a flash.

Master Dogen (1200–1253)

One of the difficulties in practice is not seeing the impermanent nature of existence. Somehow we think things will never change, and that we will be stuck with whatever we dislike forever; alternatively, we think a particularly wonderful state of affairs will never end. Expecting things to be the same, we are unable to adapt to changing circumstance.

For example, we become attached to pleasant things, circumstances, and people. By so doing, we build up a world of preferences, insulating

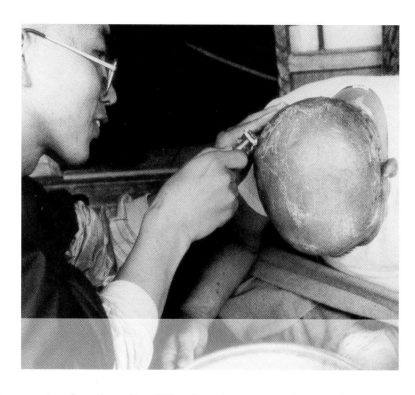

A Zen monk has his head shaved.

ourselves from the reality of life. When circumstances change and we can no longer maintain our preferences, we become lost and vulnerable.

To understand impermanence, we have to understand that no aspect of our life is fixed; that basically anything could happen. Tomorrow you could be a millionaire, or conversely the world could be destroyed. It is important not to rely on circumstance but to appreciate the life occurring now. By entering into all circumstances without fixed views, we can have a lot more latitude in which to operate and to make decisions. We will be making decisions based not on self-centered prejudice but more on what is best for the given situation, and those involved. By being open to change we can fluidly move through life without always having to exert our will over the outcome.

Parental mind

Just as parents care for their children, you should bear in mind the whole universe.

Master Dogen (1200–1253)

The practice of parental mind, or magnanimous mind, requires a broader view of life, a view that treats the world as our own body, an intimacy that is beyond our self-centered desire. An example of this parental mind is taking care of community property, town, church, and family, knowing that all benefit from it, including yourself. The narrow view would be: since I don't own it, let someone else look after it. There are many examples of parental mind in our culture, of people benefiting society when there seems very little in it for themselves. In reality, we never stand apart from our environment. If people, animals, or things suffer abuse, we suffer too. Even governments are seeing the interconnectedness of countries and environments.

Practicing in this way, we experience the intimate relationship between ourselves and all things and our sense of alienation is forgotten.

Boredom

> **A monk said to a master, "I am bored with following my breath." The master grabbed him and pushed his head under water. Just when he was about to drown, he pulled up his head and said, "Are you bored with breathing now?"**

In Zen practice, we do things repetitively; at first, as we get to know ourselves on a more intimate level, practice is new and exciting. After a while, we can get tired of the effort, and want things to move faster, to move along at the speed of our expectations. One of the mind's favorite tricks is to crave new and forever different experiences, not seeing that every experience is in fact new and vital. This usually arises out of our inability to pay sufficient attention to what is happening right now. We get blasé about life, and miss the miracle going on right now, beneath our feet.

Once Koryu Osaka Roshi was asked to participate in early experiments in biofeedback. They tested the ordinary man-in-the-street with the sound of bells. After an initial peak response on the meter, their responses began to flatten out with each strike on the bell. When Koryu Roshi was wired up to the machine, he had the same initial response, yet with subsequent strikes on the bell the response was the same, indicating his attention was always on the present moment. He wasn't bored with the repetition: Koryu Roshi at that time had been practicing for 50 years.

We all go through boring periods in our lives, yet if attention is focused, we can begin to develop new interest in life itself. We can discover how much is actually happening in any given moment, rather than just in exciting times.

Desire

Someone once asked Maezumi Roshi, "I want too much. What should I do?" Maezumi Roshi replied, "You don't want enough. You should have the desire to save the whole world."

Maezumi Roshi (1931–1995)

Desire, as we know, is the driving force of life, a force that can imprison or liberate us. Understanding desire and where it leads us is essential to Zen practice. Before we begin to practice, we usually think that we will become satisfied through chasing the object of our desires: a new car or house, better food, a more attractive mate or more of them, or more power. After experiencing the fact that the new car is now boring, the new mate has lost his/her novelty, and the additional power has added responsibilities, we are no longer satisfied and go off chasing satisfaction in more and better ways or in greener pastures.

Somewhere along the line, we become tired of this cycle, known in Buddhism as the Wheel of Samsara, and we go looking for something that will bring us satisfaction of a more lasting kind, maybe peace (nirvana). It should be noted that this is still our old friend desire. At first, we may seek the trappings of religion, robes, books, cushions, beliefs, status; yet that still does not satisfy our desire, for we have just transferred desire into the spiritual realm, and developed spiritual materialism. To move on from this place, we need to refine our approach. Now we try to experience desire and see how it feels rather than acting on it. Through experiencing desire in this way, we begin to learn how to use it in such a way that it does not hinder us.

The most common desires are food, sex, money, power, and sleep. If we did not desire food, we would die. If there were no desire for sex, there would be no human race. Without sleep we would go crazy, and power and money enable societies to function. Basically there is nothing wrong with desire. It is just that we need to learn to use it in skillful ways, not being dependent on having the object of our desires fulfilled at will.

By focusing desires to the things we know really satisfy us, then fulfillment can be achieved. Desire is a remarkable tool when applied to spiritual practice. The desire for enlightenment or for peace is fulfilled through practice, and beyond enlightenment, desire helps to further clarify life. The Ox-Herding Pictures are a wonderful depiction of the process of channeling desire.

Emotions

A famous Zen Master's favorite student had died. At the funeral service, the master was weeping copiously. His attendant was perturbed and asked, "You are a great Zen master, you are supposed to be free from attachment. Why are you crying?" The master replied, "If I don't cry now, when will I cry?"

We all have emotions and, depending on culture, upbringing, gender, and circumstance, the ways of being with and expressing those emotions will naturally vary. However, there is nowadays a tendency for people to distance themselves from their emotions, preferring displacement activity like watching television, rather than being involved in their feelings. However, if a traumatic event occurs, it is natural to feel sad and the closer the experience is to our own lives, the more intimately it is felt. This sadness washes away frustration and loss and lets us start again.

Anger is an emotion of particular interest to practitioners of all levels of experience. This is because it is such a powerful emotion and one that can cause an awful amount of damage, both to oneself and others. One of the Buddhist precepts is "Do not be angry," yet for most of us anger raises its head often. It is essential, however, when anger arises, not to push it away, denying its existence, but to experience it without action. Being with anger is not pleasant, but through experiencing it, we find out firstly what its nature is. Secondly, we can experience it and begin to understand it. Thirdly, we find out how it can be expressed in such a way that it doesn't cause damage, and ways in which it can be used to clarify a situation.

Often when angry, we find an object or person on which to vent the anger. We then curse it/him, telling it/him in no uncertain terms why they shouldn't exist, quite often ignoring our part in the whole affair. If the anger gets too strong and we cannot contain it, we lash out. Initially, lashing out feels good; yet in the long run, we nearly always regret it.

Fortunately, with experience of handling anger, we find that we can sit still in the midst of it and even continue to function rationally. In this circumstance we can determine our part in the event and even suggest a solution, instead of flying off the handle. As practice progresses, we can become adept at communicating our anger without causing damage, or at least doing as little damage as possible

If anger is channeled, it can become a great catalyst in practice. Instead of letting it fly all over the place, you can use it to clarify where you stand. Using it in such a way lets hindrances to practice be cut away. In Buddhism, anger is regarded as one of the three hidden virtues. If it is experienced rather than feared—tamed, if you will—anger can become the penetrating eye of wisdom, and the clarifying force of practice, letting you see things just as they are.

Fear

There's nothing to fear except fear itself.

President Roosevelt

Fear comes up from time to time in practice: natural fears based on difficult situations or fears arising from upbringing or self image. Again, the key to working with this emotion is to experience it. In some ways, this is true. We don't like to be afraid, so we avoid scary situations; yet only by going through these scary situations does the fear begin to dissipate. Not facing fears quite often results in phobias. By facing fear over and over, its paralyzing grip on us diminishes until we are no longer blocked by fear; we simply wear it out.

In difficult situations, we make them worse by letting the mind run wild. Thinking that it will never get better, that we will become paralyzed, that if we can't get out we will die. The monster gets bigger and bigger until we believe it and it becomes difficult even to function. In reality, we have to deal only with the present moment, and this we can always handle. Fears range from extreme physical danger to fears of meeting people and going outdoors, yet all require the same momentary attention. A friend who is a rock climber says that, when climbing difficult routes, the fear really brings him fully alive in the present moment.

Fear is also a natural response to circumstances. A Zen practitioner who flew F14 fighters from aircraft carriers, said that every time he flew night missions onto carriers he was afraid, yet it was that fear which helped him to concentrate his mind so that he could do the job and maintain a healthy respect for such a dangerous predicament. By facing fear, we liberate energies and develop capacity to operate in many circumstances, without needing to escape.

Once, someone asked the Buddha, "What is the greatest gift that you can give someone?" He replied, "The gift of no fear." This is the ultimate extension of the study of fear. Completely letting the world in, not being afraid for oneself.

Schemes and Trackless Practice

In terms of relating to the world, practicing the precepts and the Paramitas (see p.55) is a good interface with daily life. Developing love, compassion, wisdom, patience, energy, and concentration all help in experiencing unity in the world. Embodying the precepts helps us to see how much we want to escape our responsibilities as Buddhas, helping us to see the consequences of our actions and make things flow more smoothly. Reflecting on one precept for a while, a day, a week, a year, will help to break up old habits which bind us and free those energies for other things. The habits that are the hardest to break are the ones which change us the most, simply because we have to invest so much effort into uncovering their dynamics. Because of this great effort, we become more tolerant of others' difficulties, maybe even love them for their human quirks.

Ultimately, Zen practice is not about schemes or techniques, it is about living. I would often ask Maezumi Roshi, "How do I take practice into daily life." He would shake his head and say, "Just do it." At first, I didn't appreciate that advice because I felt there had to be a short cut or a trick. The shortcut is to realize practice and realization is always where you stand, and peace of mind always resides here, not anywhere else. So the trick is to come back and experience the nature that you always are; the nature that isn't proscribed by race, gender, or species, but is this vast experience that is beyond description.

To study the Buddha way is to study the self.
To study the self is to forget the self.
To forget the self is to be enlightened by the myriad things.
To be enlightened by the myriad things is to free one's
    body and mind and those of others.
No trace of enlightenment remains, and this
    traceless enlightenment is continued forever.

Eihei Dogen, 13th century

Monastic Zen

Buddhist monastic practice has developed to enable practitioners to experience enlightenment, its manifestation, and to ensure its transmission to future generations. Monasticism allows full and part-time practitioners to devote all of their time and energy to the practice of the way. In general, most monasteries are open to people who want to experience a period of intensive practice to help ground them in their daily lives. During the long history of monasticism, the monasteries have also functioned as centers of learning, and spiritual and cultural centers.

Zen monasteries evolved from their Indian counterparts, viharas. During Shakyamuni Buddha's lifetime, properties were donated as practice centers. As they grew, it became necessary to create rules, regulating how people interacted, what they did and when, and rules were needed concerning hygiene in large groups. These regulations were designed to promote harmony in the community, and thorough investigation of the Way.

Just before Shakyamuni Buddha died, he gave permission to scrap many of the minor rules, but the rules remained in place. The monasteries remained well-regulated institutions.

When Buddhism came to China, the Vinaya containing most of the rules and regulations was left untranslated until the 4th century A.D., leaving the Chinese some latitude in forming their training centers. It was not until Tao hsin (Doshin, 580–651), the third Chinese Zen patriarch, that a settled community was established. Tao-hsin had 500 monks in residence, and compiled manuals of discipline and meditation for his students, many of which had precedents in the Tien tai (Tendai) school of Chi-i. No physical record of these regulations survives today. By the time of Pai Chang (Hyakujo, 720–814) little had changed, many different Buddhist practices occurring under the same roof and pretty much the same organization. Hyakujo introduced a new set of monastic regulations dealing with hygiene, respect for elders and juniors, how to deal with troublemakers, official monastic positions, work, meals, use of halls, and the character of the abbot. Hyakujo's rules were lost, but were referred to 150 years later in the *Regulations of the Ch'an school*.

The oldest existing set of monastic rules linked with the Zen school is the *Ch'an-yuan ch'ing-kuei*, (rules of purity for Zen monasteries). Compiled in

1103 by Chang-lu Tsung-tse, a Zen abbot, it was intended to serve as a new edition of Hyakujo's rules. It was, in fact, a compilation of regulations observed in Zen monasteries of his day. It included a description of the duties of thirty monastic officers, ritual procedures for ceremonies and religious practices, and rules concerning the conduct of monks. Within a century of its introduction, these rules were widely accepted and adopted in major monasteries in China. Both of the pioneer Japanese Zen masters Eisai and Dogen were influenced by this collection when they wrote their rules (shingi). Obviously they were affected by these rules during their stay in China, and wanted their beneficent effect to be felt in Japan.

In master Dogen's rules (the *Eihei shingi*), he devotes about two-thirds of the book to encouraging stories about monastic officers who fulfilled their tasks under difficult circumstances. The message is that we don't have it half as bad as those ancient practitioners, so if we really put ourselves into it, we can attain better results. Dogen again was trying to put forward the spirit of Zen first; if the spirit can be engendered, then the rules are secondary, they become no problem. The remaining third was devoted to rules and procedures. A third generation successor of Master Dogen, Keizan Jokin, wrote the *Keizan shingi* as a companion book to the *Eihei shingi*. Master

Zen monastic practitioners: the kyosaku (awakening stick) is delivered as a sharp whack to the shoulder area if the practitioner invites the monk carrying the kyosaku to do so. This is useful for reviving one's concentration if tiredness creeps in.

Keizan had a very broad practice base, including two branches of the Rinzai School, an exoteric branch of the Tendai School, and esoteric shingon, and he studied with several teachers in Dogen's lineage, eventually choosing to continue just Dogen's line. His rules helped integrate Zen into Japanese culture, focusing mainly on calendar events (daily, monthly, yearly), and ceremonies for the emperor, local lords, and ancestors. These companion volumes are used extensively in Soto Zen today.

About 150 years after the death of Chang-lu Tsung-tse, monasticism declined in Japan, in both the Soto and Rinzai schools. The tendency was to move from centralized monasteries into smaller groups centered around a teacher. In China there had been large national monasteries with a national sangha (Buddhist community). In these monasteries, the practices were diverse, including many different sects of Buddhism. In Japan the political situation was different from that of China, Japan being a loose confederation of autonomous states, built around local feudal lords. The Japanese Zen monastic system seemed to reflect the political situation of the day, with local monasteries being supported by the local aristocracy and people, with no national organization. The monastic tradition continued its decline until the end of the 16th century, when a Chinese sect, the Obaku School (named after the mountain, not the master), revitalized the communal monastic life. They re-introduced a set of regulations known as the *Daily life of the assembly*, originally compiled in 1209. Both the Soto and Rinzai sects, threatened by the popularity of these newcomers, had to reflect deeply on what they were doing and how they were practicing. In the Tokugawa period (1603–1868), the Soto and Rinzai groups widely studied these Chinese texts, and strived to revive the Sung-dynasty style of monastic practice, involving large training monasteries. These efforts, and the many efforts of the masters of that period, ensured the strong monastic practice in Japan can still be felt today.

With the transmission of Zen Buddhism to the West, training centers are springing up in the United States and Europe. The character of these training centers is different from their Japanese counterparts. They are adapting to the culture and economic conditions of their host countries, yet at the same time maintaining the essentials of Zen Buddhist practice.

AIMS OF MONASTIC PRACTICE

In Shakyamuni Buddha's time, the word for monk was translated as home-leaver. In Japan it became *Unsui*, literally "cloud water," the monk being as free as a cloud and fluid like water, filling any situation that life brings along. The word monk has many Christian connotations that don't quite fit the Zen model. The word monk comes from the Greek word *monos* and its original implication was to be alone. Alone has a dual implication. The first is that when you are alone, you can devote all your energies to realizing your true nature. The second implication is that the monk stands alone, his/her life being the life of the whole world, not some guarded private life.

To be able to devote one's time to realizing the meaning of life, one needs a lot of support. One cannot just leave home and have everything work out happily ever after.

Monasticism was developed so that like-minded people could practice together, in such a way that most of their time could be spent in religious practice. The example of senior practitioners rubs off on juniors, and the enthusiasm of juniors rubs off on seniors, and duties can be shared among the community so that the focus remains on formal practice.

The schedule is organized enabling 24-hour practice. The duties are varied so that the monastery does not become a retreat of quietism or escapism, rather teaching flexibility, regarding all activities as practice. The rules and regulations promote harmony amongst practitioners and keep verbal communication down to a minimum; as human beings, we seem to create a lot of trouble with our mouths. Reducing verbal communication to a minimum helps us to value other types of non-verbal communication, such as body-language, how we work together, how we do things, how we hold ourselves in silence, and how we deal with emotional states. In the West, adequate verbal communication is encouraged as part of communal practice.

When a group of people gather together to practice one thing, the effect is remarkable. Take as an example the world's athletes getting together for the Olympics, and the amazing standards of athletic prowess that this promotes. The same is also true of Zen practice: when the group focus is on awakening from our own illusions, a tremendous power is generated. If the rarity of the opportunity is appreciated, then the desire to awaken cuts through any obstacles. There are a couple of quotations from monastic verses that highlight this sentiment. The first verse is usually chanted at the end of the day during training period:

Let me respectfully remind you,
Life and death are of supreme importance.
Time swiftly passes by and opportunity is lost.
Each of us should strive to awaken, awaken,
Take heed, do not squander your life.

The second verse is chanted at the end of the week as part of the *Nenju* ("10 names of the Buddha") service.

I respectfully announce to everyone,
Since the Parinirvana of the great master Shakyamuni Buddha
*   24 hundred and [insert the number of] years have passed.*
When this day has passed our days of life will be decreased by one.
Like fish living in a little water what kind of comfort or
*   tranquillity can there be?*
Let us practice diligently and eagerly as if extinguishing a fire
*   upon our heads.*
Let us contemplate impermanence and not squander our actions...

As you can see, the practitioner is urged to wholeheartedly engage in realizing his/her true nature, and not spend the time in vain. As one contemporary teacher said, "If you want to waste your time here, you'd enjoy yourself far more wasting it on the beach."

Throughout history, there has been criticism of monks who have entered monasteries and treated them as safe havens—places where they can get enough food, where they have a roof over their head, where they don't have to work so hard, and where they can retreat from the pressures of the world. There has always been this kind of person, and probably always will be; when too many people gather with this attitude, then the monasteries decline. Yet with sincere practice the monastery thrives, just like a healthy business when its people are motivated.

The monastic schedule is designed so that the place doesn't get too easy and attract people with little aspiration and determination.

THE SCHEDULE

Schedules vary from monastery to monastery and from season to season. Traditionally the year is divided into four parts. Two training periods, summer and winter, and two interim periods, spring and fall.

The reasoning behind this is illustrated in the analogy of tempering a sword. When a sword is forged, it is tempered by heating it up and hammering it, yet it is not heated so much that the edge becomes brittle. Then it is plunged into cool water and allowed to cool thoroughly, then the whole process starts again, and is repeated over and over. Training uses the same process: if you have intensive training all year round, the result would be burnout or prolonged dullness. So the schedule is made more intense during training period so that all one's energy can be focused on the practice, and cooled down during the interim period, so that the trainee can relax a little and broaden their practice and perspective, which is considerably narrowed down during training period.

TRAINING PERIOD
(Ango [Soto] or Seichu [Rinzai])

Whenever a trainee enters a monastery, there is a period of *tangaryo*—that is, a period of sitting in meditation while his/her request is processed and accepted. This period usually lasts for a day to a week; during this time, the student can reflect if their resolve is enough to carry them through monastic life. After this, the student is usually admitted. A training period traditionally lasts for 90 days and there are days of relaxed schedule on days with a 4 or a 9 in them, i.e. the 4th, 9th, 14th, 19th, 24th, and 29th of each month. This oriental system allows for four days of intense practice in-between relaxed days and it is much easier to maintain the intensity in this kind of schedule, than in a "six day on, one day off" schedule. In the West, however, we sometimes use a seven-day rotation, especially if near a population center where people come on the weekend.

During the training period, there are also weeks or weekends where the schedule is further intensified by adding more za-zen (sitting meditation) and cutting free time to a minimum. These periods are known as sesshin (to unify the mind).

SESSHIN

Yasutani Roshi once said, "Sesshin is like a battle between big mind and small mind. It is up to you how it turns out."

During this period, the rules of the center are more strictly enforced and little distraction is permitted, trainees being urged to exert their utmost efforts to realize their true nature. The atmosphere of sesshin is powerful, serious, and sincere, and there is a vitality that is experienced nowhere else. With less sleep and long periods of za-zen, the mind becomes concentrated and the body relaxed. Za-zen is practiced from eight to twenty hours a day; on the last night practitioners often sit through the night. During this period of focused za-zen, the student experiences many states of mind, and learns to accept whatever arises. Realization may spontaneously occur during times of deep absorption when the discriminative function of the consciousness quiets down. When sesshin has finished and the hardship of little sleep and long sitting are over, the body and mind are relaxed, like having completed a marathon in which you put everything into the running.

CEREMONIES

The word ceremony is derived from the Latin word *caeromonium*, its root meaning "to cure". The original implication of the word "ritual" in the English language was "to put right." In line with these two root meanings, ceremonies are performed to set our lives back into balance. We forget how truly miraculous this life is, how much there is to it, and how profound it is. We get caught up in our own petty, self-centered concerns and forget to appreciate the life that we have. Ceremonies help us to remember who and what we are, and allow us to attempt to express the inexpressible. Because much of the ritual is based around gratitude, it provides us with an opportunity to express that, and to extend the gratitude into other aspects of our life.

There is nothing magic in ceremony; there is no reward from performing these ceremonies day in and day out. The true value is through giving them life, putting forth the spirit and intention for each service. When this is done, the value becomes apparent. Then the rest of your life takes on the value of ceremony. Washing the dishes, making coffee, and cleaning the toilet are also ceremony.

Ceremonies in the Zen sect, especially in Soto Zen, are group efforts with many people participating in service positions. The services are regarded as a bridge between za-zen and everyday activities. The services have complex cues involving bells and choreography; this is an excellent form of meditation in action.

In all Zen temples there are ceremonies; these vary from temple to temple. An example of morning service, usually held after morning zazen, would be the *Maha Prajna Paramita Heart Sutra* dedicated to Shakyamuni Buddha and other enlightened ones. The second would be *The Identity of Relative and Absolute*, dedicated to the lineage of successive Buddha ancestors. The third chant, the *Enmei Jukku Kannongyo* or *Daihishin Dharani* is for our family ancestors and friends. The fourth chant is for those who are sick and for the prevention of calamity; the *Shosaimyo Kichijo Dharani* or parts of the *Lotus Sutra* are chanted. A Dharani is an ancient chant that in many cases is now untranslatable. The most important aspect of chanting a Dharani is in making the sound of the seed syllables—in layman's terms, putting yourself into the Dharani and enjoying singing.

After these initial four regular chants, there may be a special service held for a particular Zen master, either ancient or contemporary, someone like Bodhidharma. These memorial services are held on a monthly basis.

Traditionally, in the Soto sect there are three services a day. The other two are held at noon and at suppertime. The noon service could be a chant like the *Buccho Sonsho Dharani*, and the evening service the *Daihishin Dharani*, although in the West there is a movement to chant verses that have been translated into the native language.

The yearly schedule is further broken up with special services commemorating founders, Shakyamuni Buddha's birth, death, and enlightenment; and various ceremonies for ancestors. Usually, community members from outlying towns will be invited to help celebrate these memorials.

THE TEACHER

The teacher has always held an important position in the Zen school. In a Zen monastery the student usually has a strong connection with the resident teacher, and tries to work with him/her closely. Because of the emphasis on transmission through the lineage, the student needs the approval from the master before they can teach.

The teacher functions much like a guide: one who has walked the path before and has fallen into most of the pitfalls associated with practice. More importantly, he/she knows how to climb out of these pitfalls, and has enough everyday life experience to communicate this to others.

The teacher works with the student on a daily basis, and not only sees the student in formal interviews (Dokusan, Sanzen, Daisan) but will also work with him, do certain communal cleaning tasks together, and see how he/she functions with others. In this way, a more accurate picture of the student becomes available. The teacher can then work with the student on many different levels of practice. When the basic training is completed, most of the obstacles to practice are gone and methods to work with character flaws are in place. By this time, the student's practice and realization should be in accord with the standards of the tradition.

"Being in a monastery is like living in a goldfish bowl." That is the way it seems to many trainees; everyone can see what you are doing, and there is very little space to do your own thing. Traditionally, the monks would all sleep in the same room that they do za-zen in. After a while, you get used to it, and stop wanting to do the things that cause you trouble. Information very easily gets back to the teacher, who uses every opportunity to work with daily life occurrences.

Formal interviews are held every day. These meetings with the teacher, sometimes called face-to-face meetings, are one of the most important facets of Zen training. If the student is working on koans, then each time he or she enters, the koan must be presented with live words not just explanation. An example of a famous koan is "What is the sound of one hand clapping?" After a while, this becomes difficult, especially if no answer can be found. The student has to stop relying on working the koan out intellectually and take a leap, trusting his direct experience implicitly. The teacher can be very tough, and is often affectionately called "Mr. No" after his favorite word. In time, the student becomes unstoppable: no matter how many times the teacher rejects his or her answers, the student just tries harder and keeps coming back like weeds, until he/she is finally successful. Koan study itself takes many years, as there are up to 1500 koans to master—more if necessary, but usually less. When a student thoroughly penetrates one, then the rest of koan study is simple; as long as the teacher finds fault in the student's direct expression, he will keep pressing the student to fully penetrate the koan.

If the student is doing shikantaza (just sitting meditation), the focus is on how they are manifesting in daily life. The more the student can accurately describe what is going on with them, the easier it is for the teacher to help. The teacher in most cases has to rely on his/her intuition to set the student back on track. In time, a very intimate bond develops between teacher and student, yet this bond is not based around dependency but around independence and standing on one's own feet. If the student is too dependent, then it is difficult for them to stand alone once the teacher is gone. It is said that the teacher's most profound teaching is when he or she dies.

WORK (Samu)

The buildings and soil protect the Dharma and bring peace to all...

Quotation from a Zen verse.

I am not trying to tell you to discard completely quietistic meditation and to seek specifically for a place of activity to carry on your practice. What is most worthy of respect is a pure koan meditation that neither knows nor is conscious of the two aspects, the quiet and the active. This is why it has been said that the true practicing monk walks but does not know he is walking, sits but does not know he is sitting.

For penetrating to the depths of one's own true self-nature and for attaining a vitality valid on all occasions, nothing can surpass meditation in the midst of activity.

Master Hakuin, 1685–1768

Work holds an important place in Zen training, especially here in the West where most monasteries are responsible for their own survival. There is no state sponsorship and Buddhism has not been widely accepted into Western cultures, so the base for donations is small.

From Master Hakuin's quotation, it can be clearly seen that he valued this meditation in the midst of activity. It is not so good if the only time you feel good about your practice is when you are sitting in meditation. After all, our life contains many different activities, and if we can practice in only one or two, much of our life slips by while we long for those comfortable times.

The monastery is divided into two wings, the training wing and the administrative wing. The trainees are available to be assigned duties during the work periods, but the administrative wing has to take care of business whenever it arises.

In the monastery, there are many different tasks that need to be done in order for the monastery to function properly. It says in one of the meal verses, "First seventy-two labors brought us this food; we should know how it comes to us." In a large monastery in the Golden Age of Zen (618–906), there were apparently seventy-two officers overseeing the work,; everyone's efforts enabled the officers to eat. Although today there are not necessarily seventy-two officers, there are still the same kinds of work.

A Zen monk sweeps leaves at Eihei-ji temple.

The cook (Tenzo) still has an important role; everyone has to eat. The cook's role is a particularly difficult one, as meals have to be cooked on time, most of the time up to the minute. There are three meals a day, so the cook cannot sit the same schedule as everyone else. They also have to know how many people are in the monastery, how many visitors will stay for meals, who will be missing meals because of other duties, who is sick and needs a special regime, and what kind of work will be done, so that the quantity can be more accurately estimated. All this is done with the least waste possible, having deep appreciation for the food. Master Dogen said, "You should take care of the food with the same care you take of your eyes."

A Zen monk returning to the kitchen with rice pots and kettles after morning meal.

One day, Master Seppo went to practice at a mountain monastery. Before he arrived there, he stopped to get a drink of water downstream from the monastery. As he bent down to take a drink, he saw a lettuce leaf floating down from their kitchen. He turned around and walked away, saying, "The training at this monastery is too weak." In other words, they were not paying enough attention to what they were doing, and appreciating what they had. All the monastic positions require this kind of attention, to the point where the work becomes an art. All things have life and it is important not to squander it.

Duties in the monasteries are rotated regularly, fostering an understanding of each person's position and an ability to let go of attachment to favored positions. In winter everyone wants to work in the kitchen, in summer everyone wants to work outside. In letting go of these preferences, we become free to take on any task when necessary. Of course, there are some tasks that cannot be so easily rotated due to skill level, or the amount of training required.

The monastery functions very much like a business, having a treasurer, an administrator, a facilities head, a guestmaster, a secretary, a gardener, a membership director, and a program director. The teacher's role is very broad, taking care of the vision of the center, the local and distant members, and many different functions involving fund-raising and diverse contacts. Basically, the teacher or abbot does whatever is necessary to ensure the smooth functioning of the center.

Through working together, we learn a lot about each other and our idiosyncrasies. Working together is another form of communication and group awareness.

At this point, it is worth mentioning *takuhatsu* or begging rounds. In Asia the begging rounds are very important to a monk's practice. It shows her/him the interconnectedness of all things, how he/she is enabled to practice through the generosity of the people. Also, it requires a loss of ego to ask for people's support through begging. In Western culture there is a stigma against begging, and when Buddhist communities have attempted it, it did not work. In the place of takukatsu, fund-raising functions have become our begging rounds.

A monk asked Master Rinzai, *"When the sixth Ancestor was pounding rice, he lost himself. Tell me, where did he go?"* Master Rinzai replied, *"He was drowned in a deep spring." Indeed, work is the Buddha's work!*

CONCLUSION

Although monasteries have played an essential role in the maintenance of the Buddha's teaching, it is still unclear what that role will be in the West. We are now experimenting with different forms of monastic practice, involving monks and laity, male and female all practicing together. People have always gathered together for intensive practice, and it is the intensive practice that maintains the Buddha's teaching and encourages all.

Zen Culture

INTRODUCTION

From the Kamakura era (1185–1336) onward, but especially during the 13th–15th centuries, Buddhist monasteries, particularly Rinzai Zen monasteries, played a major role in the cultural as well as spiritual life of Japan. Zen monks, out of their austere practice and emphasis on non-attachment and on being as opposed to becoming, brought a new esthetic to Japanese cultural arts, architecture, food, and martial arts. Senior Zen monks had a high standing in military and court circles. The Abbot's quarters of Zen monasteries became places of learning and cultural exchange, while the monks were themselves welcome in the homes of nobles, warriors, and men of culture. The influence of Zen thus spread throughout medieval Japanese society.

In this chapter, we examine the relationship between the Zen tradition and the tea ceremony, gardens, the domestic Japanese house, calligraphy and ink painting, haiku, and Japanese food. We devote a separate chapter to the influence of Zen on the Japanese martial arts.

THE TEA CEREMONY AND TEA GARDEN

Tea is nought but this.
First you make the water boil,
Then infuse the tea.
Then you drink it properly.
That is all you need to know.

The tea ceremony (*cha-no-yu*) was originally practiced by Zen monks, but it has so permeated the esthetic culture of Japan that it now—perhaps of all Japanese cultural pursuits—best encapsulates all the strands of Japanese spiritual and artistic sensibilities. The specific qualities associated with the tea ceremony are simplicity, restraint, and naturalness. At its deepest level, cha-no-yu, literally "hot water for tea," aspires to create such an atmosphere of harmony and tranquillity that the participants may experience the same feelings in their own hearts and minds.

The ritual drinking of tea was introduced to Japan by the Zen priest Dai-o in 1267, but it did not become important in Japanese culture until the Muromachi period. Under the Zen master Ikkyu (1394–1481) and particularly later under his pupil Shuko (1422–1501), it developed into an elaborate cult especially among imperial court circles and the high ranking warrior classes. Shuko taught the art of tea to the Ashikaga shogun Yoshimasa (1435–1490). The tea pavilion built for Yoshimasa in the grounds of Ginkaku-ji Temple (originally the Silver Pavilion) in Kyoto became the defining model for all later tearooms. In 1485 Yoshimasa became a Zen Buddhist monk and after his death the Silver Pavilion became a Zen Buddhist temple. Following the shoguns' enthusiasm, the tea ceremony and its devotees became ever more influential in Japanese society. However, the rituals surrounding it became increasingly elaborate and luxurious and this finally provoked a return to simplicity and austerity.

The reaction was initiated and led by the Zen priest Sen no Rikyu (1521–1591), who devised a set of rules governing the tea ceremony that still apply today. Rikyu saw that the ceremony had lost its original meaning and had become an empty ritual reflecting only the taste and politics of court life. He emphasized a return to simplicity, not only of the ritual but also of the setting and the utensils used. The rules he established for the classical tea

Students of Zen archery at the Enkakuji Temple in Kita-Kamakura finish their three-hour lesson with a tea ceremony.

ceremony were based on four principles: harmony, reverence, purity, and silence. He stressed simplicity and rusticity, but within a framework of beauty and naturalness. His style came to be known as Wabi-cha, rustic tea.

Rikyu's approach was inspired by the spirit of Zen. This Zen sensibility is illustrated in a story told by A. Sadler, a well-known chronicler of Japanese culture, in his book *Cha-no-Yu*: "Once a certain person came to Rikyu and asked him what were the mysteries of Tea. 'You place the charcoal so that the water boils properly and you make the tea to bring out the proper taste. You arrange the flowers as they appear when they are growing. In summer you suggest coolness and in winter coziness. There is no other secret,' replied the Master. 'All that I know already,' replied the other with an air of disgust. 'Well, if there is any one who knows it already, I shall be very pleased to become his pupil,' returned Rikyu."

The spirit of Rikyu's approach is perfectly caught in Koto-in Zen Temple in Kyoto. Koto-in has a beautiful Zen tea garden and three buildings, one of them a tea house. The temple is a masterpiece of elegant simplicity (especially renowned for the beauty of its maple trees in the fall).

Koto-in was established in 1601 at the behest of a famous military leader, Hosokawa Tadaoki. Hosokawa was a great warrior of his time and one of the few to survive the bloody civil war, which culminated in the establishment of the Tokugawa Shogunate. In addition to his martial skills, he was a man of considerable intellectual achievement and an accomplished diplomat. His wife, Lady Grate, was a devout believer in the then outlawed Catholic faith and her father was the disgraced leader of an unsuccessful revolt against the then shogun. Hosokawa overcame this potentially fatal association and became a prominent figure in the early Tokugawa regime. He was rewarded with vast domains of land, but later in life devoted himself to the study of Zen under the famous Daitokuji abbot Seikan (1588–1661). He was also noted as one of the most distinguished disciples of Rikyu.

Shoko-ken, one of the three buildings in Koto-in, is the teahouse built by Hosokawa but inspired by the teachings of Rikyu. Shoko-ken, reached by a stone flagged path across a small inner landscaped garden, has a tiny kitchen for washing the vessels used in the ceremony and a *tokonoma* (alcove) decorated with an elegant *kakemono* (hanging scroll) and a simple vase with simple flowers. It complies perfectly with Rikyu's rules for the tea pavilion. The *chaniwa*, or outer tea garden, also has all the traditional chaniwa features; it is designed to enhance the peaceful, spiritual nature of the tea ceremony, hence such a garden's description as the "fourth wall" of the teahouse. The one at Koto-in displays ferns, moss, evergreen trees, and shrubs, set against bamboo fences and stone lanterns. The visitor moves through the chaniwa and toward the teahouse along stepping stones placed asymmetrically on the ground. He or she then encounters a *machiai* (waiting room), separated from the inner garden around the teahouse by a *chumon* (small gate). Within the inner garden, there is a stone water basin, used to wash hands and rinse the mouth before entering the teahouse. Lord Hosokawa and Lady Grate are buried in the garden, their grave marked by a stone lantern.

Rikyu later in his life became a favorite of the warlord Oda Nobunaga (1534–1581), and after his death, of shogun Toyotomi Hideyoshi (1536–1598). Hideyoshi was a most influential ruler and, in his enthusiasm for tea, he even took time out for the tea ceremony during military campaigns. This ensured the ceremony's continued popularity. Rikyu also served as Hideyoshi's advisor and it was thus his view of the form and meaning of the tea ceremony that prevailed in court circles and therefore society at large.

Sadly, Rikyu was obliged to commit suicide by Hideyoshi in 1591. What happened is not totally clear but in his book *The Whole Japan Book*, Boye De Mente tells the poignant story as follows: The roving eye of the Taiko (Great Person), as Hideyoshi was called, also fell upon Rikyu's beautiful daughter. But Rikyu refused to send her to his master, thus incurring his wrath.

Apparently reluctant to attack the famous tea master directly, Hideyoshi bided his time. Sometime later, Rikyu was accused of putting a statue of himself in the temple of Murasakino. Hideyoshi accused him of gross arrogance, unbefitting the grand master of tea, and invited him to commit hara-kiri.

A request from the taiko was a command. Rikyu, then in his 70th year, asked to be allowed to conduct one more tea ceremony before taking his own life. His request was granted—and the ceremony is said to have been one of the best the old master ever conducted!

ZEN GARDENS

A young novice Zen monk, told to tidy a garden, asked his master where he should throw the rubbish. "Where is the rubbish?" asked the master as he took broken twigs and leaves for kindling and carried small stones to catch rain drips from the eaves, leaving only a small pile of dust and gravel which he raked back into the garden. That is all you need to know.

The introduction of Zen Buddhism into Japan during Kamakura era had a significant impact on garden landscaping. This influence is initially associated with the book *Emposho (Book of Gardens)*—written by the Zen priest Zoen, it is one of Japan's earliest and most influential books on garden design. Zoen emphasized tranquillity and harmony rather than variety and decorative qualities. The influence of the Zen ideal has continued to the present day and many of Japan's most celebrated gardens have been designed by Zen priests and created within the grounds of Zen monasteries and temples. Here they provide the monks with a contemplative, everyday work activity, an esthetic experience, and a place of natural beauty.

Compared to the Western garden, the Zen garden is subdued, with the stress on spatial harmony instead of geometric form. For example, when the famous Zen gardener Muso Kokushi (1275–1351) laid out the gardens of Saiho-ji Temple, Kyoto (popularly known as the Moss Temple) in the 14th century, he did not flatten the ground but instead let the moss follow the natural undulations of the surface. With twenty varieties of mosses, he created a range of contrasting and complimenting shades of green. Trees and stones were then planted and placed subtly among the moss to look quite natural. Stepping stones, in contrast to the straight gravel paths of the West, were spaced irregularly. In the best Zen gardens the work of the gardener is ideally unseen.

Economy of means is another characteristic of the traditional Zen garden. Rocks, sand, water, trees, shrubs, ferns, and moss are the basic components used to represent mountains, rivers, lakes, and waterfalls and, out of them, create scenic landscapes in miniature.

Daisen-in temple garden, Kyoto.

The deeper underlying philosophy of the Zen gardener, however, is to demonstrate a reverence for life and nature and to let the observer experience the fundamental reality of all things. Out of this Zen view and the natural landscape at hand, three styles of Japanese garden evolved: the *tsukiyama* (landscape or pond/sea/hill style), the *karesansui* (rock or waterless stream), and the *chaniwa* (tea garden, see page 136).

The tsukiyama style of garden typically features streams with stepping stones and a bridge leading to a small island set in a pond. A twisting path leads the visitor from one feature to another, so that various changing scenes can be viewed. Some gardens feature miniaturized versions of actual beauty spots famous in Japanese art or literature. One variation of the tsukiyama style of garden is known as the *kaiyu* or "many pleasure" style. Popular with the *daimyo* (feudal lords) of the Tokugara Shogunate, the kaiyu style features several gardens built around a central pond. Often, one or more of them incorporates views which lie outside the garden itself, a technique known as "borrowed views" (*shakkei*) or "capturing alive" (*ikedori*). This feature is often seen in gardens in the Kyoto area, where the spectacular mountains that surround the city are seen framed by gateposts and trees.

The Saiho-ji (1339) and Tenryu-ji (1343) temple gardens in Kyoto are noted examples of the tsukiyama style. Both were designed by Muso and are still preserved in their original form. In both gardens he gave symbolic expression to the ideal land of Zen as described in the *Hekiganroku*, a Chinese book of Zen often used as the basis of *teisho* (Dharma talk by a Zen teacher) within the Rinzai tradition. The gardens are places of visual beauty, but Muso also intended to design them as physical manifestations of the great truths expressed by the Ch'an masters.

Muso lived as a wandering monk seeking enlightenment until the age of fifty. On his wanderings, he established many small mountain temples with gardens incorporating the natural scenery. In later life, he was patronized by the Ashikaga shoguns and Emperor Go-Daigo and appointed abbot of the monasteries of Tenryuji and Rinsenji. Toward the end of his life, he withdrew to the small temple of Saihoji, where he created his famous moss garden.

In the karesansui or rock garden style (also called dry stone landscape) few shrubs are used and the most common elements are stones, sand, and gravel. They are designed, like a painting, for contemplation. Several of the best Zen gardeners were also well-known painters in ink, and in this medium they intended, with just a few strokes of black ink on white paper, to evoke an atmospheric natural scene. Their gardens were three-dimensional evocations of the same idea, using sand or gravel instead of silk, and shrubs, trees, or stones instead of brush strokes. The stones they chose were also charged with different meanings according to their shapes, their textures, and the angles at which they were placed.

The garden at Ryoan-ji Temple, Kyoto (completed 1513) is generally recognized as one of the finest examples of a karesansui in Japan. It is said to have been created by Soami (1472–1525), a famous ink line artist (some dispute this). The garden consists of an expanse of raked white gravel with 15 stones in three groupings. A mellow earthen wall and monastery buildings frame the whole. Perspective is achieved through variation in the size of the rocks and the way the gravel is raked. The garden is said to symbolize the manifoldness of the world. Some suggest it represents a group of mountainous islands in a great ocean, others a tigress leading her cubs across a stream. In the spirit of Zen, however, it is finally left for each observer to arrive at his or her own understanding of the garden.

Soami was an official painter in the court of Yoshimasa, the eighth Ashikaga shogun. In 1480 he designed and built one of the earliest and, most famous Zen stone gardens for the abbot's residence at Daisen-in, a sub temple of Daitokuji Temple, Kyoto. At the time, Soami was influenced by Chinese Sung period paintings which, by their portrayals of dramatic and awe-inspiring mountain landscapes, emphasize human vulnerability. His garden at Daisen-in, designed to be viewed from the veranda of the abbot's quarters, rather than to be walked around, is constructed of rocks and sand. Unlike the abstract garden of Ryoanji Temple, it is a three-dimensional representation of a Sung-style painting featuring a mountain (Mount Horai, the mythical home of enlightened beings), a river, and a boat with a cargo of treasure. It has been suggested that the garden may be seen as a representation of the bridge between being and non-being.

Like other Zen gardens, Ryoanji and Daisen-in were designed to promote the meditative practice of Zen monks. Rock and sand gardens, unaffected by the changes of the seasons, were said to provide the monks with a sense of the calm of eternity.

THE JAPANESE HOUSE

The qualities and characteristics attributed to traditional Japanese architecture such as simplicity, restraint, harmony with landscape, purity, the use of natural materials, and a feeling of rusticity and unpretentiousness are very much those admired within the Zen tradition. This is not a coincidence, since the design of Zen temple buildings, with their emphasis on plainness, serenity, and cleanliness, had a profound effect on the development of Japanese architecture. This is particularly so of the traditional Japanese house, whose design was very much influenced by the esthetic sensibility of Zen temple buildings, especially the living quarters of Abbots and other established priest classes. To exemplify the qualities of the Japanese house and its relationship to the Zen ideal, we reproduce here a beautiful and knowledgeable description written for us by the American architect Richard Smith, who lived and taught for many years in Japan.

The traditional Japanese house is built with a relatively small number of well-known and locally available materials. House construction does not usually rely on remote industrial processes and because building components are not apt to be transported great distances, environmental pollution caused by all forms of transport is reduced.

"Zen Buddhism teaches that the transformation of appearance through weathering or age in both animate and inanimate things is to be honored—being both beautiful and morally right. Translated into the language of architecture, a weathered wall communicates that both beauty and morality reside in the simple, commonplace, and unadorned. It is, perhaps, a major consequence of this Japanese attitude toward materials and life that in a Japanese house the need for surface embellishment and preservation is considered unnecessary, and so the amount of toxins entering the domestic environment is reduced.

There is a profusion of objects and spaces in the Japanese environment, which are at once useful and beautiful, and which communicate a spiritual message. For instance, stones in a garden wall are chosen for their differing shapes and sizes and then carefully fitted together to ensure structural integrity and a beautiful composition. At the same time, they graphically embody a sense of community made up of individual parts—a spiritual and symbolic message.

The overhanging roof of the Japanese house, in its shape and expansiveness, is symbolic of shelter and affords great protection, not only to inhabitants but also to the materials with which the house is built. These reduce the harmful effects of weathering, caused by sun and rain, upon the delicate and vulnerable materials used to construct inner walls. Again, the need for protective coatings, with their associated hazards, is reduced.

The whole of the house is placed a certain distance above the ground, enabling ventilation of the under-floor space and reducing dampness within the house. The structure is also protected from mildew, damp, and decay.

Cleanliness is generally understood to be fundamental to good health. In Japan, house-"keeping" is ultimately associated with house-"cleaning" and it must be a preoccupation of the occupants if the high standards of sanitation and health expected of a good householder are to be maintained. To this end, the Japanese home contains several more or less standardized features which contribute to the maintenance of a clean and healthy house.

The *genkan* (entrance hall) is sometimes referred to as a vestibule, but it does more than act as a draft lobby. The genkan consists of a floor, which is at the same level as the garden, plus a raised floor level. You sit on the raised wood floor to remove shoes before donning slippers and moving elsewhere in the house.

Many visitors do not proceed past the genkan, thereby reducing the intrusion of dirt into more private areas of the house. No animals pass the genkan, though they may sleep there and find shelter from the elements. Consequently a large amount of dirt is left in the genkan, where it can be readily removed into the street or garden.

You move in slippers on wooden floors to the inner matted rooms, which must be entered with bare or stockinged feet. The street, the genkan, the wooden corridors, and the matted rooms represent four levels of decreasing contamination between public and private places. The exclusion of dirt from the matted living rooms is important, as the floor is the eating and sleeping surface. Because less dirt enters the house, less cleaning is needed.

The *engawa* (veranda) is a well-protected porch that provides a place for work and relaxation in the sun and fresh air. Its overhang and disposition afford shelter from the sun during the summer, while letting the lower winter sun penetrate into and beyond it. Also, the large opening of the engawa lets massive quantities of air circulate through the house, even during heavy rain. Because the engawa is connected to a garden, this air may be seen to be conditioned by its passage through vegetation and over green ground cover, stones, sand, etc, which may be wetted down to reduce the intrusion of dust. Like the genkan, the veranda floor surfaces are easily maintained and their nearness to the garden facilitates cleaning in general.

Symbolically, the engawa is the link between house and garden. In Zen monasteries, it may be used as a platform for za-zen meditation. The absence of furniture in the Japanese house facilitates the flow of air. *Futon* (Japanese bedding) is simple, easily cleaned, and unobtrusive. Essentially similar to the European duvet, futon are easily folded twice and placed in cupboards designed to contain them. Futon are aired frequently in the engawa and the natural contents may be "plucked up," increased or decreased, or replaced as desired. Futon are beautiful, warm and, by their number and pattern, reflect the age, status, and taste of their users.

Tatami (floor mats) are located in all major rooms. They are resilient and cushion falls. Because one sleeps on this firm floor, support for the back is good.

Sitting on the floor requires considerable discipline and muscular control to achieve acceptable comfort and grace in movement and posture. Putting on and taking off shoes, turning in limited spaces, operating sliding doors carefully and from several positions, bowing deeply and respectfully, and other such activities contribute to an awareness of bodily disposition and constitute a form of exercise akin to balletic movement. It is all quite beautiful, symbolic, and healthy.

Rooms are arranged and re-arranged according to how they need to be used, esthetic effect, convention, or whim. Nothing is permanent or finished. The empty rooms are like theatre stages—ready for the next scene and equipped accordingly. This requires almost constant "scene changing"—the moving about of props, careful lighting, and costume changing.

The Japanese have an attitude toward building and living that is akin to the art of gardening. Houses are constantly "tended." In the hot and humid summer, all sliding-panel room dividers can be opened or removed, encouraging the flow of fresh air throughout the house. This provides a healthy response to climate.

In the winter, the rather loose association of open rooms with large openings to the outdoors can be converted to an arrangement of isolated

Kiyomizu Temple.

rooms which can be closed off from each other and the outside by sliding panels and outside shutters. Outer rooms become "buffers" to the inner rooms.

There is no central heating system, although *hibachi* (small transportable braziers) burn charcoal for direct radiant warmth. Because the house is well ventilated, summer and winter, danger from the accumulation of harmful gases is reduced but, still, great care and skill in firemaking and tending is required.

Families gather about the *kotatsu*, which is a hibachi placed below floor level, over which a table is placed. This feature is equivalent to the Western hearth, and is symbolic of family unity. During cold weather, hot tea is drunk in cups without handles, which warm the hand and mouth.

To live well in the Japanese house, considerable reliance is placed upon appropriate dress in both summer and winter. The *yakata* is a lightweight, heavily starched, loose, cotton garment worn in the summer, which allows free circulation of air next to the skin. In the winter, however, it is traditional to wear layers of heavier garments. Their full sleeves allow hand warming and, in a sitting position, the surface area is reduced and bodily heat more

Byodoin Temple.

efficiently retained. Clothing becomes a heavily insulated, personal tent—the first line of environmental defense against hypothermia.

Bathing, in addition to making a contribution of its own to personal cleanliness and good health, is another way of keeping warm and conserving body heat. The *ofuro* (bathtub) is a relatively deep and short bath. The water is heated from its own boiler, usually located outside the house. You wash thoroughly before entering, sometimes with others, to soak. The bath water is, therefore, kept clean, reused and reheated when necessary. Boards can be floated to insulate the water and prevent excessive heat loss.

The bathing method ensures a very hot, clean, and relaxing experience. It can be a social occasion whether at home or at the *sento* (public bathhouse). Immersion in high-temperature water over a considerable time has a meditative dimension and is symbolic of ritual cleanliness and religious purity. After the bath, one's body is warm and, once under the futon, the effect seems to continue throughout the long winter night.

In the traditional Japanese house, the washroom, lavatory, and bathtub are not associated in the same room. They are regarded as separate and distinct activities requiring separate space. The bath is frequently associated with the garden and contains enough room for several people to dress in an atmosphere of architectural and natural beauty and social ease. It is a place where it is comfortable to be exposed and to relax.

The lavatory is sometimes entered only upon leaving the house. It is sited carefully to reduce noisome odors and social embarrassment. The WC compartment is well ventilated and may contain a flower arrangement.

The urinal is sometimes located in the garden. This outdoor placement of sanitary appliances enables more convenient movement to new and uncontaminated places and ensures that living in the house provides regular and frequent use of the garden at all times of the day and night and during all seasons. This may have a marked affect upon psychological well-being, social harmony, and the appreciation of art and nature, which is at the root of Japanese religious and philosophical thought.

Like so many characteristics of Japanese Zen life, civilization in general and the Japanese house in particular, activities are performed in a natural manner or setting. The Japanese house does little to separate its occupants from the outdoors. One is largely exposed to the sweeping and subtle changes of nature daily and with the seasons. Perhaps the greatest lesson of the Japanese house is to remind us that we, in the West, have distanced ourselves from a more natural and healthy place in the world. The industrialization of virtually all aspects of life and our apparent desire to manifest every new technological or scientific idea or advance in the fabric of the home, may play a larger role in our health and well-being than we dare think.

Okakura Kazuko in his *Book of Tea* tells an apt story: Rikiu was watching his son Shoan as he swept and watered the garden path. "Not clean enough," said Rikiu, when Shoan had finished his task, and bade him try again. After a weary hour, the son turned to Rikiu: "Father, there is nothing more to be done. The steps have been washed for the third time, the stone lanterns and the trees are well sprinkled with water, moss and lichens are shining with a fresh verdure; not a twig, not a leaf have I left on the ground." "Young fool," chided the tea master, "That is not the way a garden path should be swept." Saying this, Rikiu stepped into the garden, shook a tree, and scattered over the garden gold and crimson leaves, scraps of brocade of autumn! What Rikiu demanded was not cleanliness alone, but the beautiful and the natural.

CALLIGRAPHY AND INK PAINTING

Calligraphy (*shodo*), the "way of writing," is perhaps the most highly regarded art form in Japan. As a skill, it has been prized for well over a thousand years and for much of that time a person's character and cultural achievement was judged by the beauty of his or her writing.

Shodo is written (painted) with a brush using *sumi*, an ink made from lampblack or soot mixed with glue, then dried and compressed into sticks. The stick is rubbed with water on an *inko* to make liquid ink. The brushes are made in different sizes and thicknesses. They have bamboo handles and tips made from animal hair.

Shodo is difficult because the brushes are not easy to use, the paper soaks up the ink, and correcting mistakes is impossible. Further, the beauty of the writing is considered an integral part of the message. Master calligraphers teach that the key to shodo is to do it not just with the hand but with the whole body and mind in unison and yet to be simultaneously spontaneous and free.

Such an approach appealed to the Zen ideal and within the Zen tradition there developed a calligraphic style called *bokuseki* or "traces of ink." Bokuseki written onto paper scrolls is traditionally hung during the tea ceremony. The characters might be admired as abstract forms or designs for their own sake, as well as for the message conveyed. Their beauty lies in their shape, position, the gradation of the ink, and the nature of the brushstrokes. The calligrapher aims to imbue the strokes with his own personality and, by connection, his state of mind will also be manifested in the writing. Thus a Zen master and calligrapher through his brush strokes illustrates his state of being.

Ink painting (*sumi-e*), a style of monochrome painting that also uses black sumi ink applied with brushes onto paper or silk, is an art form related to calligraphy and one that has been especially practiced by Zen monks. Initially it

was they who brought to Japan mastery of the Chinese Sung dynasty ink-painting style (*suibokuga*). Later, however, during the Muromachi Era (1337–1568), the Shogunate patronized Zen and its related arts and in this period ink painting became established as a major, widely practiced Japanese art.

A modern Chinese master of Zen painting, Qui Zhenping.

The most common Zen subjects in ink painting are landscapes on Buddhist subjects, including Bodhidharma and other hermit monks. The paintings are often mounted on vertical hanging scrolls called *kakemono*. They tend to be stylized and allusive, their intention to transcend the form and yet reveal its very essence or suchness. To go with the painting, poetic inscriptions are often written in the corner by the painter. Their content and style is judged as one with the picture. A famous Chinese painter of this school, K'un ts'a, said: "Speaking of painting in its finest essentials, one must read widely in the documents and the histories, ascend mountains, and trace rivers to their sources, and only then can one create one's ideas."

ZEN POETRY (Haiku)

*A haiku is the expression of a temporary enlightenment
in which we see into the life of things.'*

(R.H. Blyth)

Haiku is a highly stylized and refined form of Japanese poetry that
traditionally deals with nature and human life. The poet attempts to present
a fleeting glimpse of what he has seen or felt in an elegant, spare way. In each
haiku, it is also customary to refer to a flower, animal, event, or other matter
that will evoke the feeling of a particular season or, by association, a human
emotion; for example, cherry blossom and the brevity of life. Haiku often
identify the self with the creative spirit of nature.

Haiku was developed in the middle of Japan's Edo period in the late
17th century by Matsuo Basho (1644–1694). Basho is considered the founder
and greatest exponent of haiku in its present form. Basho took the opening
verse of a long-established linked verse form called *haikai-renga* and made it
into an independent form. Haiku poetry came to consist of seventeen
syllables arranged in three lines, the first and last line of five syllables and
the second line of seven syllables. It is a form that is said to be both the
simplest and the most difficult in Japanese poetry.

Basho's most famous poem came to him when he heard the sound of
the water as a frog jumped into a pond. He wrote:

*The still pond, ah!
A frog jumps in:
The water's sound!*

Two other well-known examples of his haiku follow:

*The sea dark
The call of the teal
Dimly white*

> *Soon it will die*
> *Yet no trace of this*
> *In the cicada's screech*

Basho moved to Edo (near Tokyo) in 1672. He gained a reputation as a poet and teacher, but was deeply bothered by religious doubt. He studied Zen, but never became a monk. Instead he decided to travel and journeyed throughout Japan. Basho published poems, journals, and sketches describing his travels. His best-known work and one translated into English is *The Narrow Road to the North* (1694).

Through Basho, haiku became a very popular poetic form, not only in Japan but in foreign countries as well. This has been the case particularly since the early 20th century, when his poems were first translated into English and French. Here is a selection of contemporary haiku by the Welsh poet and author, Ken Jones.

> *Kamakura*
> *77 temples*
> *and not a single Laundromat*
>
> *Awakened*
> *by clappers and doves*
> *white light on the shoji*

(Clappers summon Zen monks to meditation)
Kyoto and Kamakura, spring 1997

> *Stillness of trees*
> *silence of sheep*
> *winter twilight*
>
> *In the darkness*
> *first cock crow*
> *beat of my heart*

Solo Retreat, winter 1977, Meirionydd, Wales

Haiku is now, like Zen, widely practiced in the West. There are many magazines devoted solely to it in England, Ireland, and America, where contemporary *haijin* may have their poems published.

ZEN FOOD

Though our modern lives are full of comfort, we have gradually become distant from our natural environment. Living in homes with heaters and air conditioners has isolated us from the changes in the four seasons. We tend to forget the gentle breeze in the treetops and the warm rays of the sun. Shojin cooking emphasizes rather than hides these delights. On a cold and snowy day in winter, one sits hunched over, warming the tips of one's fingers on a steaming bowl of soup. And in the summer's heat there are cold noodles on a bed of ice and deep green leaves. Or one can enjoy cold, white tofu as it floats in clear water.

Soei Yoneda, Abbess, Sanko-in Temple

Correct food preparation and good dietary practice form an integral part of Zen training. The philosophy of food preparation in a Zen temple includes the idea of cooking for spiritual development and its purpose is to contribute to the physical, mental, and spiritual health of the cook and those who eat the food. The underlying principle is the very simple one of love and gratitude for the food received.

Preparing food in the frame of mind recommended by Zen masters is an extremely difficult task and it requires the cook to be totally present for the job. Perhaps giving all our attention to the simplest tasks is the wisest way to start: "When washing rice, focus attention on the washing and let no distraction enter."

Zen cook and priest Keizo Kobayashi, in his book *Shojin Cookery*, describes how a balance of seasonal qualities is sought by considering the five methods, the five colors, and the five flavors. These sets of five refer to the five positive roots of good spiritual practice—faith, meditation, energy, wisdom and memory. The five methods refer to the different ways of preparing food: boiling, grilling, frying, steaming, and serving uncooked food. The five colors are green, yellow, red, white, and black (purple is considered black for this purpose; e.g. eggplants). The five flavors are shoyu, sugar, vinegar, salt, and spices. The most commonly used spices in shojin cookery are ginger root, sesame seeds, and wasabi, a Japanese mustard. By balancing these three sets of five variables, the Zen cook aims at making a vegetarian meal that is appropriate to the season and ingredients as well as nutritious, delicious, and lovely to look at.

Shojin cookery had its origins in China, and the philosophy underlying it was taken back to Japan by monks who had been to China to study Ch'an. One of the most famous of these was Dogen Zenji, who wrote two treatises on the subject: *A Guide for the Kitchen Supervisor* and *Instructions for the Zen Cook*. They became reference works in many Zen monasteries and the principles extolled also influenced more general developments in Japanese cooking. A number of the unique characteristics of traditional Japanese cuisine have their origins in shojin ryori.

In his book *Instructions for the Zen Cook*, Dogen carefully explains the qualities to look for in choosing the cook or tenzo for monastery duties. He says, "Tenzo duty is awarded only to those of excellence who exhibit faith in Buddhist teachings, have a wealth of experience, and possess a righteous and benevolent heart. This is because tenzo duty involves the whole person." Further, he says that if a person entrusted with the job of tenzo lacks such qualities or the spirit for the job, then they will endure unnecessary hardships and suffering and the work will have no value in their pursuit of the way. The job of cook, as far as Dogen is concerned, is obviously a serious one.

The same sentiment is expressed by the Chinese monk Zongze (1102), who wrote a ten-volume work called *Regulations for Zen Monasteries*. Ten volumes! He tells the tenzo to "put your awakened mind to work, making a constant effort to serve meals full of variety that are appropriate to the need and the occasion, and that will enable everyone to practice with their bodies and minds with the least hindrance." (See *Refining your Life*, translation by Thomas Wright).

In the book *Good Food From a Japanese Temple*, Soei Yoneda describes the Zen cook's job in very practical terms: "It is imperative for the tenzo to actively involve himself personally in both the selection and the preparation of ingredients."

The tenzo also inspects the rice as it is washed, in order to ensure the absence of sand or grit. This he carefully discards, but not without being on constant guard for even one grain of rice that might be mistakenly wasted. He at no time lets his mind wander as he cleans the rice. The tenzo also concerns himself with the "six tastes" and the "three virtues" (*rokumi santoku*). The six tastes are bitter, sour, sweet, hot, salty, and "delicate," and the tenzo works to balance these effectively, while also incorporating the three virtues of lightness and softness, cleanliness and freshness, and precision and care. In so doing, he expresses the spirit of shojin cookery. A balance of the six tastes and the three virtues happens naturally when, in the cleaning of the rice, the washing of the vegetables, the boiling in the pot, and in all the other aspects of the cooking process, the tenzo commits himself totally and directs his attention to nothing else but the work at hand.

In an interview, Abbess Koei Hoshino, Soei Yoneda's successor, when asked what shojin-ryori meant to her, replied: "Shojin is my way of staying alive, that is all. There is nothing harmful in it, which is important. I eat the food to sustain me. Mind you, the food we eat ourselves on a daily basis is simpler than that served to our customers. After a hard day's work, one does not long for delicacies. The simple yet delicious tastes of a bowl of rice gruel with pickled plums, or of rice just off the stove accompanied by miso soup are unforgettable."

Asked what basic advice she gave to the lay cooks who came to her for training, she said: "Firstly and most importantly I tell them to concentrate fully on what they are doing; secondly they must not make a mess; finally nothing should be wasted. For instance, here we use the peelings from carrots and other vegetables to make pickles for the next day's meal."

The motto of the Sanko-in Temple, which nowadays serves food to the public on special days as a way of raising funds, is *chori ni kometa aijo*, which means "cooking with love." When asked whom this love was for, Abbess Koei Hoshino replied: "This love is for Buddha nature, for the people who eat our food, for the ingredients, and for the pots and pans. In fact, the essential flavor of the food comes from one's heart, from cooking with one's whole soul, and from respecting the spirit of the kitchen. Also we love the crockery we use and try not to make a noise with it when we eat. It takes a novice about three years of study to learn how to handle her eating bowls correctly. Only then will she be ready to start to learn shojin-ryori."

Asked what simple advice she would give to an ordinary person who wished to lead a life of spiritual endeavor, the Abbess said: "Whatever you do, you must put your whole heart into it. Practice this day after day. That is enough. Here, for instance, we believe that if we put all our energies into making the best possible food we can with the best possible taste, then we are pleasing Buddha. A meal reflects the gentle nature and warm heart of the cook. Of course, some of us are more clever with our hands than others, but if one does the best one can, a fine meal results almost as if by divine grace."

Finally, in response to a request for a tip for the Zen cook, she replied: "In shojin cuisine we try to harmonize the five tastes: sweet, salty, vinegary, bitter, and hot, plus one more which is also very important. That is the soft taste, as of tofu, for instance. Once finished eating, one should be left with this perfect soft aftertaste. Remember that if the first sip of a meal is perfect the aftertaste will not be, so one must strive for subtle, developing flavors

rather than those with a strong, immediate impact on the taste buds. Taste and texture, preparation and nutrition are all important in achieving this perfect balance."

Shojin cookery is also sometimes referred to as *yukeseki*, or medicine. This embodies the same principle as that contained in the Indian ayurvedic medical system. In this school of thought, food selection and preparation are seen to be inseparable from the treatment of disease and the cultivation of good health. The traditional Chinese medical view is the same thus, "If one

Abbess Koei Hoshino
in her kitchen at Sanko-in
temple, Tokyo.

falls ill, one should first examine one's diet, then choose well, chew carefully, and give thanks. In this way, the curative powers of nature with which mankind is blessed are given full rein to act and nearly all diseases are conquered."

The Zen diet is traditionally vegetarian and a practitioner abstains from eating all flesh foods, except in particular defined circumstances. This vegetarian practice is based on the Buddhist precept of non-killing of all sentient beings, which recognizes the interdependency and oneness of all life.

Before each meal, the Zen practitioner recites a sutra. There are different ones for different times of the day or season or particular occasion, but the *Gokan no be* or *Five Reflections Before Eating* is heard at most meals. *Gokan no be* is chanted in a variety of forms, but they all have the same message. Here is an extract from a version chanted at the midday meal:

LEADER: **We offer this meal of three virtues and six tastes to the Buddha, Dharma, and Sangha and to all the life in the Dharma worlds.**

ALL: **First, seventy-two labors brought us this food; we should know how it comes to us. Second, as we receive this offering, we should consider whether our virtue and practice deserve it. Third, as we desire the natural order of mind to be free from clinging, we must be free from greed. Fourth, to support our life, we take this food. Fifth, to attain our Way, we take this food.**

The sutra is recited to remind and renew the understanding of the partakers of the food of the path of the Buddha.

The first line of the response reminds us of how much effort by very many people went into growing, harvesting, processing, cooking, and serving the food about to be eaten and how food may be grown only because of the natural gifts of sunshine, rain, and soil.

The second line asks if we have acted with enough charity, love, and effort at good practice to deserve such a gift.

The third line reminds us not to be greedy and to remember in not eating overmuch those people who are hungry.

The fourth line expresses the view discussed previously that food is a medicine needed to sustain physical and spiritual strength.

Finally, the fifth line reminds us that we eat to be given the opportunity to follow the Buddha Way and to express our Buddhahood in the world.

Zen and the Martial Arts

Following the introduction of Zen into Japan from China, Chinese priests traveled there to spread the teaching. One of these, Bukko Kokushi (1226–1286), a priest of the Rinzai sect, became the teacher of the most powerful warrior in Japan, Hojo Tokimune (1251–1284), who ruled Japan from his base in Kamakura. Bukko Kokushi was a living exemplar of the kind of courage and spiritual composure in the face of death admired by the samurai. In China, as he sat in meditation in the Noninji temple, a number of Mongol soldiers entered the building with drawn swords. Bukko sat perfectly still and recited a poem:

In heaven and earth, no crack to hide;
Joy to know that man is void and the things too are void.
Splendid the great Mongolian longsword,
Its lightning flash cuts the spring breeze.

The Mongol soldiers, perhaps impressed by Bukko's courage, left him unharmed. Obviously the ability to face death unflinchingly was of great interest to the warriors who ruled Japan, and someone like Bukko Kokushi, who was a living example of the qualities the samurai wished to cultivate, was valued greatly. Chinese monks were also valued by the Japanese warrior class, as they were considered to be experts on the Mongols, who, after their conquest of China and Korea in the 13th century were considered to be a threat to Japan.

KAMAKURA WARRIOR ZEN

The samurai knew that, once committed to battle, they would either kill the enemy or be killed. This stark choice between life and death prompted many warriors to search for methods to improve their chances of survival. Obvious lines of enquiry included improving the quality of their weapons and armor, and developing improved physical skills in the use of those weapons. But the mental composure of a warrior when facing death was also understood to be of vital importance, and anything which could strengthen a man's mind and spirit was investigated. The importance in Zen training of direct experience, rather than ritual or intellectual speculation, and the self-reliant, courageous personalities of many of the Zen masters appealed to the samurai. As Sir George Sansom explains in his book *A History of Japan to 1334*, "For a thoughtful warrior, whose life always bordered on death, there was an attraction, even a persuasion, in the belief that truth comes like the flash of a sword as it cuts through the problems of existence. Any line of religious thought that helped a man to understand the nature of being without arduous literary studies was likely to attract the kind of warrior who felt that the greatest moments in life were the moments when death was nearest." Zen, with "its simplicity, directness, and efficiency instantly won the heart of

Fierce Buddha image in painted wood, Muromachi period, 1392–1568.

the warrior, and the samurais began to knock at the monastery gate."

A school of Zen evolved in Kamakura, the headquarters of the Bakufu or military government. As the samurai were not familiar with the Buddhist sutras or the traditions and background of Chinese Buddhism, the method of Shikin Zen or "on the instant Zen" was developed by the Chinese teacher Daikaku, who arrived in Japan in 1246. He used koans derived from the normal lives of his samurai pupils. This kind of Zen has been described as "a Zen of crisis"; it was rooted in the realities of the warrior's lives, but once peace was established in the 17th century this approach almost disappeared.

While the samurai were attracted to Zen as a way of improving their fighting ability, there is no doubt that some samurai developed a profound understanding of Buddhism. When Hojo Tokimune died in 1284 at the age of thirty-three, his teacher Bukko commented on his enlightenment, saying that he had thrown off earthly desires and become a spiritually advanced soul, or Bodhisattva.

Uesugi Kenshin (1530–1578) was one of the great generals of Japanese history. The struggles he had with his great rival Takeda Shingen (1521–1573) are famous in Japanese history. A warrior steeped in Zen, which he studied under the Soto Zen master Soken, he left the following advice to his followers: "Those who cling to life die, and those who defy death live. The essential thing is the mind. Look into this mind and firmly take hold of it, and you will understand that there is something in you which is above birth-and-death and which is neither drowned in water nor burned by fire. I have myself gained an insight into this samadhi and know what I am telling you. Those who are reluctant to give up their lives and embrace death are not true warriors."

Takeda Shingen was a follower of Kaisen, the Archbishop of Myoshin-ji. He shared Kenshin's views on life and death. He wrote, "The practice of Zen has no secret, except standing on the verge of life and death."

There is a Zen-flavored story which describes a meeting that may have taken place between the two warriors. During a stalemate in one of the series of battles they fought at Kawanakajima, Kenshin rode alone into Shingen's camp, where he found his opponent sitting on a chair with only a few guards to protect him. Kenshin drew his sword and aimed a blow at Shingen's head, asking him a typical Zen question used by teachers to test the spiritual maturity of their students, "What would you say at this moment?" Shingen simultaneously parried the blow with a *tessen* (iron war fan) and answered, "a flake of snow fallen on the red-hot stove." Kenshin lowered his blade and said, "Melting and flowing into the murmuring waters of the River Sai."

TAKUAN AND THE YAGYU FAMILY

The famous swordmaster Yagyu Munenori (1571–1646) was the teacher of the third Tokugawa shogun, Iemitsu (1604–1657), and himself a student of the Zen master Takuan Soho. In a series of letters to Yagyu, Takuan made several observations that much influenced Yagyu. Takuan emphasized the point that if the mind is fixed or stopped on action, it is then impossible for the swordsman to gain victory. With reference to this, he gave Yagyu the following advice:

There is such a thing as training in principle, and such a thing as training in technique. . . If you do not train in technique, but fill your breast only with principle, your body and your hands will not function. Training in technique, when put into terms of your own martial art, is in the training that, if practiced over and over again, makes the five body postures one.

Even though you know principle, you must make yourself perfectly free in the use of technique. And even though you may wield the sword that you carry with you so well, if you are unclear on the deepest aspects of principle, you will likewise fall short of proficiency.

Technique (ji) and principle (ri) are just like the two wheels of a cart.

See The Book of Five Rings *by Thomas Cleary, which includes a translation of The Family Traditions on the Art of War by Yagyu Munenori*

In his own written work Yagyu explained that the mind of the swordsman must be free, or unattached to externals. His view was that this state of *mushin* ("no mind") gives the swordsman the opportunity to fight with total efficiency. Technical mastery has long been achieved and the ego conquered, so nothing stands in the way of a perfect performance. There is no fear of failure or desire for success; indeed, life and death have been transcended, and because of the lack of inhibition or ego the warrior survives. His mind is not troubled by thoughts of death or injury and it does not dwell or stop on technical problems. The mind in this state is said to resemble the moon reflected in a stream. The water may be disturbed, but the moon stays clear and serene, unaffected by the water's turbulence. Yagyu left a poem to one of his sons which encapsulates the essence of his teaching. It says:

> *Behind the technique, know that there is the spirit:*
> *It is dawning now;*
> *Open the screen,*
> *And lo, the moonlight is shining in!*

He further clarifies the point thus:

> There is a Zen saying, "the great action is direct and knows no rules." "Direct" means that the action of a man of full inner awareness appears directly; and the fact that the action of a man of such awareness is not bound by any of the training principles he has learned, or by any established ways of doing a thing, is expressed by the words "knows no rules." The "rules" are the training, the ways of doing, the accepted methods. For everything there are instructions, there are ways and means which are usual. But the man who has attained gives them up altogether. He acts freely and spontaneously. He who is free, outside the rules, is called a man of great awareness and great action.
>
> Awareness means never to lose inner clearness, to see in everything its real point. If this awareness congeals and grows hard by thinking and thinking, it becomes caught up in the things. This means it is not yet mature. But if practice is continued rightly, in time the awareness will become mature and fill the body, and he will work in freedom. This is called the great action.

He goes on to list the "diseases" which inhibit the development of true mastery. They are:

1. The desire for victory.
2. The desire to resort to technical cunning.
3. The desire to display all that he has learned.
4. The desire to overawe the enemy.
5. The desire to play a passive role.
6. The desire to get rid of whatever "disease" infects him.

Yagyu points out that if these "diseases" or desires are present in the mind, then spontaneous or natural responses are blocked. Of course, this produces the first problem; the desire to be rid of desires is itself a desire and so a problem: like someone trying to catch his own shadow, logic and reason create a dilemma. The swordsman (like the Zen practitioner) must solve this dilemma if he is to master the secrets of true swordsmanship.

There is a another story involving the Shogun Iemitsu, Takuan Soho (the Zen master), and Yagyu, which deals with the ability to face possible death calmly. Iemitsu was given a wild Korean tiger as a gift and he challenged Yagyu Munenori to enter the animal's cage and stroke its head. Yagyu entered the cage and slowly moved towards the tiger, keeping his gaze firmly locked on the animal, while he stretched out his hand and touched the tiger on its head. He carefully moved backward and out of the cage, gasping in relief once he was safe. Iemitsu then looked at Takuan Soho and asked if the Zen mind could match the swordsman's mind. Takuan instantly ran to the cage, spat on his palm and presented his hand to the big cat, which sniffed and licked it. Takuan quickly touched the cat on the head and left the cage. Iemitsu observed that the way of the sword cannot compete with Zen.

Another member of the Yagyu family who had direct experience of a Zen-inspired form of training was Yagyu Matajuro. As a child, he showed promise as a swordsman, but he was lazy and failed to make progress, so his family disowned him. Determined to make something of himself, he sought out a noted swordsman named Banzo, who lived near the Kumano Machi Shrine, a place famous for holy men who trained themselves by undergoing severe austerities. Matajuro approached Banzo and said that he wanted to learn swordsmanship, but Banzo showed no desire to teach him. Matajuro pleaded with him, saying that he would work hard, to which Banzo said that he might learn something in ten years. Explaining that he had only a short time to study as his father was getting old, Matajuro asked how long it would take if he totally devoted himself to training. Banzo told him that it might take thirty years. Matajuro realized that he was being chastised for being impatient, so he stopped asking questions and told Banzo that he would agree to any conditions if only he would accept him as a pupil. Banzo nodded and told the boy to move his possessions into his hut.

Matajuro spent his days washing, cooking, collecting firewood, and cleaning his master's house, but Banzo failed to teach him any techniques with the sword. After three years, he confronted Banzo and reminded him of his promise, but the master said nothing and walked away. Matajuro despaired of learning anything and decided to leave. That night, as he lay on his mat asleep, Banzo crept into his room and struck him with a wooden sword. From that point on, Matajuro's life was nothing but pain.

Without warning, Banzo would attack him with the wooden sword, striking him painfully if he was too slow to avoid the blow. In time, however, Matajuro developed lightning fast reactions and almost supernatural awareness and Banzo was unable to land a blow even when Matajuro was busy cooking rice. Without a single formal lesson, Matajuro had mastered his art, and when he returned to his home he took a fine sword and a certificate of mastery presented to him by Banzo.

Here, however, we must be careful not to over-emphasize the effect of Zen on classical Japanese martial arts. It is likely that the Zen-like style of writing adopted by Yagyu Munenori in his book is in part a deliberate imitation of Takuan's prose style, and that this had the effect of reinforcing the belief that it was only through Zen that the most profound secrets of the martial arts could be discovered. While many classical Japanese martial arts traditions drew at least some of their ideas from Zen, they also looked at other traditions such as Taoism, Neo-Confucianism, Shinto, and Esoteric Buddhism. It has been pointed out that a study of the *horimono* or engravings on Japanese sword blades shows that "over ninety-five percent of these engravings concern Esoteric Buddhism (mikkyo).....Not a single engraving concerns Zen or its concepts." While some samurai sought mental strength in Zen, others placed their trust in magic.

TOKUGAWA JAPAN

After the Tokugawa family became the dominant force in Japan by the victory of their forces at the battle of Sekigahara in 1600, the role of the samurai in Japanese society began to change. The age of the "country at war" ended and the need for ferocious warriors declined. Peace brought new problems for the samurai and so they sought a new role.

With the advent of peace, the Tokugawa shoguns looked to the teachings of the Chinese philosopher Confucius for ways to govern Japan. Two schools of Neo-Confucian thought exerted powerful influences: the teachings of Chu Hsi (1130–1200) which stressed reason (*ri*) and the ideas of Wang Yang Ming (1472–1529), who taught that intuition (*shin*) was of the utmost importance. Wing-Tsit Chan explains that "The fundamental difference between Chu and Wang lies in the fact that while Chu's approach is intellectual, Wang's is moral."

Nakae Toju (1608–1648) is considered to be the founder of the Wang Yang Ming (Oyomei in Japanese) teachings in Japan. He wrote, "There are many degrees of learning, but the learning that teaches control of the mind is the true learning. This true learning is of the utmost importance in the world and the chief concern of mankind."

One of the reasons that Wang Yang Ming's teachings appealed to the samurai was because they had much in common with Zen. According to Wang Yang Ming's teachings, true moral behavior is not produced by

conformity to laws and regulations or the fear of being punished; rather, it stems from an innate moral sense which leads the individual to act in a sincere manner.

The Tokugawa shoguns appointed Confucian advisers, who promoted the Chinese beliefs in civil government and polite learning. Hayashi Razan (1583–1657), who was an adviser to Tokugawa Ieyasu, wrote "To have the arts of peace, but not the arts of war, is to lack courage. To have the arts of war, but not the arts of peace, is to lack wisdom. A man who is of inner worth and upright conduct, who has moral principles and mastery of the arts is also called a samurai. A man who pursues learning, too, is called a samurai."

The idea that a warrior should combine both civil (*bun*) learning and military skills (*bu*) became established at the beginning of the Tokugawa period. Ieyasu Tokugawa laid down thirteen articles in 1615 called the *Buke Sho Hatto* (*Rules for Martial Families*), which clearly states that samurai should excel not only in martial pursuits, but also in literature, history, poetry, and other academic skills. Of the samurai of that time, it was said, "He was educated to be a man of wholesome character whose intellect, feelings, and will were in harmony with living a virtuous life ...Unless he successfully achieved the stipulated balance in his education, the warrior was considered a rustic, something useless, 'like a paper fan without its supporting backbone splints'."

One of Hayashi Razan's students was a young *ronin* (masterless samurai) named Yamaga Soko (1622-1685). Destined to become known as one of the "three great Ronin" of the Tokugawa period, Yamaga Soko became a very important and influential thinker and writer. He gave systematic form to the Japanese warrior's code known as *Bushido*, stressing loyalty, devotion to duty, austerity, and a willingness to die when called upon—these traditional virtues were bound together by Confucian ethics.

This fusion of civil and military learning became known as *Bunbu Ryodo*, or as the Zen master Taisen Deshimaru translates the term, "The Twofold Way." The ideas inherent in the concept of Bunbu Ryodo were vital for the development of the Martial Ways (*Budo*), where the aim of the training was no longer to simply develop combat skills but instead to educate the whole person, to develop his character to that of a gentleman in the classic Confucian sense, a gentleman who also retained the fighting skills of the samurai. This ideal was accepted by many skilled swordsmen; Miyamoto Musashi wrote, "It is said that the warrior's is the twofold Way of pen and sword, and he should have a taste for both Ways. Even if a man has no natural ability, he can be a warrior by sticking assiduously to both divisions of the Way."

A group of Japanese Samurai warriors. Many classical Japanese martial arts traditions drew some ideas from Zen.

Training in the techniques of the martial arts was seen as an austere discipline or shugyo, where the intention was to subdue the trainee's ego in order to improve his character and spiritual strength. Once again, Zen methods were adopted to assist in this aim.

Some flavor of the time can been seen in the writings of the 18th-century poet Moto Mokuami, who wrote:

Sweat dripping down
As you drill away at
the arts of the sword:
That they're no use,
May this reign be praised.

During the 16th century, Zen went into something of a decline in Japan. Zen training became so formalized that true Zen experience was relatively rare, but in the 17th century a number of teachers emerged who revitalized the teaching and practice of Zen. One of those teachers was Suzuki Shosan (1579–1655), who was born into a warrior family in the province of Mikawa. His family served Tokugawa Ieyasu, and Shosan fought in the final battles that established the Tokugawa Shogunate.

During his time as a warrior, Shosan visited a number of teachers in order to develop his growing interest in Zen. At the age of forty-one, Shosan gave up the life of a warrior in order to become a Zen monk. Many of Shosan's followers were samurai, as Shosan believed that warriors and students of Buddhism shared common virtues: courage, commitment, and an awareness of death. Shosan emphasized *shi ni narau*, or confronting death, as a way of loosening the individual's attachment to the ego. Shosan often referred to *Nio zazen* in his teaching. The Nio (also known as *Kongo Rikishi*) are two muscular ferocious guardian deities who stand at the gates of Buddhist temples. Each carries a version of a *vajra* (thunderbolt) known as a *kongosho*, which symbolizes the diamond-hard wisdom mind. To Shosan these deities symbolized the vital energy needed to follow the Zen way. Shosan said to one of his samurai followers, "From the beginning, it's best to do za-zan in the midst of strife and confusion. A samurai, in particular, must be able to do za-zen while uttering his battle cry. Guns are firing, lances are flying, you send up a battle cry. It's here that you can clearly make good use of your practice. What use can you have for the sort of za-zen that needs a quiet place? However appealing the Buddha Dharma may be, the samurai should throw out anything he can't use when the moment for his battle cry arrives. So he never needs anything but the mind of the Nio."

The "sword that gives life" (*katsujin-ken*) and the "sword that kills"(*setsunin-to*) are terms found in the *Hekiganroku* (Chi. *Pi Yen Chi* or 'Blue Cliff Records'), a collection of Zen koans and commentaries by two Chinese teachers Hsueh-t'ou Chung-hsien (980–1052) and Yuan-Wu Fo-kuo (1062–1135). The terms were used by Yagyu Munenori in his written work and according to his ancestor Yagyu Muneyoshi (1529–1606), the founder of the Yagyu Shinkage Ryu, "In our school, the sword that is positioned for attack is called the death-dealing blade, and the sword that is not, the life-giving sword." Originally these terms simply referred to methods of wielding a sword, but in time they came to have moral overtones. In 1768 Kimura Kyoho wrote the *Kenjutsu Fushiki Hen* (*The Unknown in The Art of Swordsmanship*). He says "The perfect swordsman avoids quarreling or fighting. Fighting means killing. How can one human being bring himself to kill a fellow being? We are all meant to love one another and not to kill. It is abhorrent that one should be thinking all the time of fighting and coming out victorious. We are moral beings, we are not to lower ourselves to the status of animality. What is the use of becoming a fine swordsman if he loses his human dignity? The best thing is to be a victor without fighting.

"The sword is an inauspicious instrument to kill in some unavoidable circumstances. When it is to be used, therefore, it ought to be the sword that gives life and not the sword that kills."

Hakuin (1685–1768), the great Zen master, had a passion to make Zen understandable to the common man, so he devoted a great deal of his time to teaching all who came his way. In time, he gained many followers.

One day a samurai came to visit Hakuin and asked him, "Is there really a heaven and a hell?" Hakuin looked at him for a moment and said in an insulting tone, "who are you to ask this question? You look too stupid and ugly to understand even if I did bother to answer your question." At this, the warrior became so angry that he reached for his sword. "Don't bother with your sword," said Hakuin. "You are probably so clumsy that you couldn't hit me, and the weapon is probably too blunt and rusty to do any damage even if you managed to land a lucky blow." This was too much for the warrior, who began to draw his sword from the scabbard. "Ah, the gates of hell are opening," said Hakuin in a soft voice. The samurai immediately grasped the lesson and slid his sword back into the scabbard, bowing deeply to Hakuin. "Now the gates of heaven are opening," observed Hakuin.

The samurai had learned the difference between the sword that gives life and the sword that kills.

YAMAOKA TESSHU

Yamaoka Tesshu (1836–1888) is often called the last of the great Japanese swordsmen. He is an important figure in the transmission of the martial arts of the samurai to a wider following, and representative of a generation of masters who were able to spread formerly exclusive systems to non-samurai practitioners without losing the true meaning and martial spirit.

Tesshu was born into a samurai family. His father introduced him to the art of the sword and he later became a student of the famous swordsman Chiba Shusaku, who taught Tesshu the *Hokushin Itto Ryu* style of swordsmanship. At the age of twenty, Tesshu was adopted into the Yamaoka family after his marriage to Yamaoka Fusako in 1855. He was taught the Yamaoka style of spear fighting and at about the same time he became involved in the political ferment of the young "shishi or men of high purpose." As well as studying the arts of the sword, Tesshu devoted himself to the practice of za-zen. His lifelong study of Zen and the martial arts led to the creation of his own school of swordsmanship, which he called Muto Ryu. In his own dojo or training hall, the *Shumpukan* (*The Hall of the Spring Wind*, a name taken from a poem written by the 13th century Zen master Bukko Kokushi), Tesshu taught his method to his students. He devised three tests called *seigan*, a Buddhist term that means a "vow," which could be taken only by advanced students. After a thousand consecutive days of practice, the candidate could take the first test, which consisted of 200 contests with only a short pause for food. If successful, the candidate was eligible to take the second test, which featured 600 contests over a period of three days. The third seigan was the ultimate test: 1,400 contests over seven days, which pushed the candidate into realms where physical skills were not enough. To be successful, the swordsman had to unite all his physical and spiritual strength with the attitude that victory or death could be the only choices.

Tesshu believed that, "Swordsmanship should lead to the heart of things where one can directly confront life and death. Recently, swordsmanship has become a mere pastime with no bearing on matters of importance."

One of Tesshu's students, Kagawa Zenjiro, left a record of his experience of seigan. "On the third day of these strenuous exercises, I could hardly raise myself from bed and had to ask my wife's help. When she tried to lift me, she felt as if raising a helpless corpse and unconsciously withdrew her hands, which she had placed underneath my back. And then I felt her tears on my face. Hardening myself to the utmost, I admonished her not to be so weak-hearted. Somehow I succeeded with her help in raising the upper part of my body.

"I had to use a cane to walk up to the training hall. I had also to be helped to put on my protecting equipment. As soon as I took my position, the contestants began to crowd in. After a while, I noticed one member come in and approach the master to ask his permission to take part in the exercises. The master permitted him right away. I looked at him and at once realized that he was the one noted for his rascality. He, disregarding the swordsman's usage, would thrust his bamboo sword to the naked throat behind the protecting gorget and keep it up even after he was already struck over the head by his victorious opponent.

"When I saw him coming up to me, I made up my mind that this would be my last combat, for I might not survive the contest. With this determination, I felt within myself the surging up of a new energy. I was quite a different person. My sword returned to its proper position. I approached him now fully conscious of my fresh inner surge, and lifting up the sword over my head, was ready to strike him with one blow of it. At this moment came the master's emphatic command to stop, and I dropped my sword."

Tesshu taught that the true purpose of the martial arts were as methods of forging the spirit. They were a *shugyo*, or austere discipline, whose aim was not simply the destruction of an enemy, but the development of a form of spiritual strength in the practitioner. For years, Tesshu struggled to strengthen both his body and his spirit. He overcame all his opponents and trained with such ferocity that he was nicknamed "demon," but at the age of twenty-eight he faced Asari Gimei in a match. Asari Gimei was a master of the *Nakanishi-ha Itto Ryu* style of swordsmanship, and although Tesshu attacked with all his strength, he was unable to make any impression on his opponent. He became Asari's student, but in subsequent matches he was unable to penetrate Asari's defenses, and was soundly defeated time after time.

Tesshu turned to Tekisui, the abbot of Tenryuji, for help. Tekisui gave Tesshu a koan to study and meditate on. He was told to concentrate all his efforts to understand the following:

When two flashing swords meet, there is no place to escape,
Move on coolly, like a lotus flower blooming in the midst of a
roaring fire,
And forcefully pierce the Heavens!

At the age of forty-five, while sitting in meditation, Tesshu finally grasped the meaning of Tekisui's koan. He went to see his teacher Asari Gimei to put his enlightenment to the test, but as soon as they crossed swords, Asari let his blade drop, exclaiming "You have arrived." Later, Asari designated Tesshu as his successor as the Headmaster of the Nakanishi-ha Itto Ryu.

Yamaoka Tesshu wrote in June 1880, "The essence of swordsmanship lies in mastery of the two aspects of universal and particular. Once body and mind are polished and refined, one arrives at the marvelous state where particular and universal are unified. Continue to forge the spirit and particular and universal will soon be forgotten—this is 'a single sword against the cold sky'. If you want to obtain the secrets of such wonderful techniques, drill yourself, harden yourself, undergo severe training, abandon body and mind; follow this course for years and you will naturally reach the profoundest levels."

Tesshu's "single sword against the cold sky" refers to the meeting between Kusunoki Masashige (1294–1336) and the Zen master Gokushun, which took place at a Zen monastery at Hyogo. Masashige was about to lead his troops into battle against a huge army led by Ashikaga Takauji (1305–1358). He asked the master, "When a man is at the parting of the ways between life and death, how should he behave?"

Gokushun replied, "Cut off your two heads [your dualism] and let one sword stand cold against the sky."

D. T. Suzuki explains that "The sword here represents the force of intuitive or instinctual directness, which unlike the intellect does not divide itself. It marches onward without looking backward or sideways."

ZEN AND THE MARTIAL ARTS TODAY

With the Meiji Restoration, the samurai class came to an end, and the martial arts and associated traditions went through something of a decline. Some methods, such as Judo, were restructured as sports while others became systems of exercise, or self-discipline. However, the Zen-influenced methods and values did not totally vanish, even among those systems that are predominantly sporting in intent.

Modern martial artists have been influenced by Tesshu's ideas to a great extent, and the famous karate master Mas Oyama adapted Tesshu's method of seigan to his own school of karate. Practitioners of Kyokushinkai karate can, if they wish and they are strong enough, engage in 100 contests without pause as a test of their physical and mental conditioning. Many systems of traditional martial arts have special training sessions in the depths of winter—the practitioners measure their fortitude against the numbing effects of snow, ice, or freezing water. A common practice for some karate styles is to perform the *kata* (formal exercise) of *Sanchin* (Three Battles) while standing under a waterfall fed by melting snow.

One of the first Westerners to experience any form of Zen training through a martial art was Eugen Herrigel, who studied *kyudo* (archery) under the great master Awa (1880–1939) from 1932 to 1937. Herrigel explains that, "By archery in the traditional sense, which he esteems as an art and honors as a national heritage, the Japanese do not understand a sport, but, strange as this may sound at first, a religious ritual. And consequently, by the 'art' of archery they do not mean the ability of the sportsman (which can be controlled, more or less, by bodily exercises), but an ability whose origin is to be sought in spiritual exercises and whose aim consists of hitting a spiritual goal, so that fundamentally the marksman aims at himself and may even succeed in hitting himself."

When the lawyer and student of Buddhism, Christmas Humphreys, visited Japan in 1948, he was taken to see a demonstration of judo and kendo, both of which he had practiced for many years as a member of the *Budokwai dojo* in London. He described the demonstration as "Zen Buddhism in action," and explained that "Mr. Koizumi, the founder and presiding genius of the Budokwai, is right to insist on his pupils understanding these principles, lest the physical contest, which should be a manifestation of philosophy in action, should degenerate into mere wrestling. As I found by experience, only when one achieves one's first clean throw in Judo, without thought or purpose intervening, and learns to win by giving way, which is the heart of Judo....has one found in action the spiritual heart of Zen."

The association of Zen and the martial arts is by no means over. The Zen master Taisen Deshimaru taught Zen in France until his death in 1982. He often held classes in association with highly graded martial arts masters to show the relationship between both disciplines.

In 1972 the Zen master and swordsman Omori Sogen established the Chozen-ji temple and International Zen Dojo in Hawaii as the main temple of a new line of Rinzai Zen. Chozen-ji is "a place of Zen training where persons of any race, creed, or religion who are determined to live in accordance with Buddha nature may fulfill this need through intensive endeavor." One of the means of "intensive endeavor" is by training in the martial arts, and the grounds of Chozen-ji include a most impressive martial arts dojo. In his book *One Arrow, One Life*, Kenneth Kushner recounts how he visited the Chozen-ji to pursue his study of Kyudo (archery) and the Zen way. As in all Zen temples, students are expected to contribute to the general workload. Kushner was told to clear some large rocks off a hill in order to make a path. He began by pushing as hard as he could against one of the rocks and soon became very tired, with very little to show for all his hard work. His teacher Tanouye Tenshin Roshi watched him as he fought against the weight of the stones, and then with a smile spoke to Kushner and explained that the main problem was that Kushner was trying to make the

The art of Zen archery
demands close concentration
and consistency.

stones go where he wanted them to go. "You have to learn how to push the rock where it wants to go," he said. As in Judo or Aikido, one does not attack at a point where an opponent is well balanced and strong; the attack should be directed where the opponent would be easily unbalanced. Kushner explains what then happened: "At the end of his talk, Tanouye Roshi demonstrated a way to find out where a rock 'wanted' to go. He put his hand on one edge of the rock and tipped it slowly. He then put his hand on another part and repeated this process. This continued until he had pushed the rock at several points around its circumference. Next, he showed me the point at which it was easiest to push the rock. By pushing that point, he effortlessly moved the rock in the direction it 'wanted' to go. He continued to demonstrate how, by repeating the process of pushing the rock in its favored direction and occasionally spinning the rock so as to re-orient the direction it 'wanted' to go, it was quite easy to move it where I wanted it to go."

Many instructors of modern martial arts see their training as producing something more than simply winning medals in a sporting arena. The Korean Taekwondo master Sang Kyu Shim explains that ultimately, training in a martial art "has one chief purpose: to show man his own face." This sentiment is echoed in a poem written by the founder of Aikido, Morihei Ueshiba, who wrote:

The penetrating brilliance of swords
Wielded by followers of the Way
Strikes at the evil enemy
Lurking deep within
Their own souls and bodies.

The symbol of the sword as an instrument that destroys the "enemies" within the mind of the practitioner may be seen in the images of the Buddhist "divinity" known as *Fudo Myoo*. He is usually portrayed standing in an aggressive posture, with a sword in his right hand and a rope in his left. Fudo Myoo represents the clear mind, free of all delusions and illusions, and his sword is the instrument that cuts through ignorance.

When the Okinawan martial art of karate became established in Japan in the 1920s, it quickly absorbed elements deriving from Zen. The characters used to write karate changed from "China Hand" to "Empty Hand." The character for "empty" *kara* (also read as *ku*) taken from the expression *ku soku ze shiki, shiki soku ze ku* ("form is emptiness, emptiness is form") found in the *Prajnaparamita Hridava Sutra* (The Heart Sutra).

The founder of Shotokan karate-do, Gichin Funakoshi, explained that, "Just as it is the clear mirror that reflects without distortion, or the quiet valley that echoes a sound, so must one who would study Karate-do purge himself of selfish and evil thoughts, for only with a clear mind and conscience can he understand that which he receives."

Funakoshi studied Zen at Engaku-ji temple in Kamakura, and in 1968 a memorial to him was erected in the grounds, with an inscription that reads: *karate ni sente nashi* (there is no first attack in karate).

Zen in the West

The mind of the Great Sage of India has been intimately conveyed from west to east.

Identity of Relative and Absolute (Sekito Kisen, 700–790)

As we begin the third Millennium, Zen has definitely taken root in the west, especially in the USA. At this point, most of the original pioneer Japanese Zen Masters have passed away and the teaching is almost exclusively in the hands of their Western successors, although there does appear to be another wave of Japanese teachers, both Soto and Rinzai, visiting this country. Some are merely on teaching visits, others settle permanently.

The whole spectrum of training centers is in place, from sitting groups to local temples, city centers, mountain centers, and monasteries. The types of Zen available are also varied, from Korean and Vietnamese to Chinese and Japanese and the lineages are diverse.

Along with this, American Zen is being molded by many influences from other Buddhist schools, such as the Theravadan and Tibetan, and Western religions such as Christianity and Judaism. Cultural influences also play an important part, plus popular influences such as psychotherapy and self-development work. Women have been very influential in the establishment of Zen in the USA. In Asia, because of the position of women, this was not so.

HISTORY

In 1854 Commodore Perry, accompanied by two fully armed steamships, landed in Japan and forcibly negotiated a treaty that effectively opened Japan up to foreign influences. By 1893 the first Zen Master, Soyen Shaku, set foot on American soil after being invited to attend the World Parliament of Religions in Chicago. This one journey had profound effects on western Zen.

Before 1854 Zen could have been transmitted through the Chinese Zen Buddhists. However, most Chinese priests seemed interested only in catering to ethnic Chinese and taking care of their temples. It seems that sincere monastic practitioners did not leave China (or at least there is no record of them doing so).

 Much of the groundwork for Zen pioneers was done by the Buddhists in the Theosophical Society, especially Madame Blavatsky and Colonel Olcott. The latter visited Japan in 1888 and voiced the need for Buddhist practice in the west.

 The first public Zen talk was given by Soyen Shaku at the world Parliament of Religions. It was translated by a young scholar called D.T. Suzuki, and was read by Dr. John H. Barrows. The title of the talk was 'The Law of Cause and Effect as Taught by Buddha.'

 After the parliament Soyen Shaku stayed at the house of Dr. Paul Carus who was to invite Shaku's student, D.T. Suzuki, to translate several Buddhist works including Ashva-Ghosha's The Awakening of Faith in the Mahayana. Because of his background in practice D.T. Suzuki's translations did much to encourage several generations of Zen Practitioners and provided much-needed material for study.

 In 1905 Soyen Shaku returned to the USA to stay for nine months at the home of Mr. and Mrs. Alexander Russell of San Francisco. Accompanying him was Nyogen Senzaki, a young monk who had trained at Soyen Shaku's temple, Enkakuji, with D.T. Suzuki. One evening when walking through Golden Gate Park Soyen put down Senzaki's suitcase and said, "This may be better for you instead of being hampered as my attendant monk: just face the great city and see whether it conquers you or you conquer it." He said goodbye and disappeared into the fog. Senzaki never saw him again. This was the start of Nyogen Senzaki's teaching career in the new world. He studied all the English books on Buddhism he could find. However, as Soyen had instructed, he did not even write the "B" of Buddhism for seventeen years.

 In 1906 Sokatsu Shaku, a successor of Soyen, came to the USA with six of his disciples, one of whom was Sokei-An Sasaki, who remained in

Madam Blavatsky (1831–91), who introduced Eastern religious philosophies to the West in the 19th century and founded the Theosophist Society.

America. They bought 10 acres of land near Hayward, California and attempted to set up a Zen Community based on farming. Unfortunately, the land had been overworked. They struggled for a year producing strawberries, but they couldn't compete with their neighbors. When they brought the produce to market a market supervisor said, "What do you call these, schoolboys?" "Strawberries," they replied. He showed them a fist-sized strawberry and said, "Now this is a strawberry. Better take that stuff to the piggery." That was the end of the farming Zen Community. By the following spring, the farm was abandoned and the group moved to San Francisco, where they offered their place as a venue for a sitting group that they called *Ryomokyo-kai*. About 50 Japanese students and some Americans attended, and a young monk called Goto Zuigan translated for them. (Zuigan later became Abbot of Daitokuji).

Sokei-An wandered around America until 1919, doing many different jobs. One hot July day he passed the bloated carcass of a dead horse on the street. Seeing the horse awoke in him the impermanence of his own life, so he went home, packed his bags, and resolved to complete his studies with Sokatsu Shaku. He went back and forth to Japan for nearly 10 years, completed his studies, and was certified to teach independently in 1928.

Sokei-An later became a monk, believing that no one would take seriously a layman teaching Zen in America. His teacher disagreed with him, and the two never spoke again. He returned to New York penniless and homeless, yet by 1931 he had signed the incorporation papers for the Buddhist Society of America, and had eight students attending.

By 1938 the group had thirty people and some were working on koans. Sokei-An was in no hurry to build up numbers, as it had taken four hundred years for Zen to take root in China. He likened the difficulty of the enterprise, and the patience required, to "holding a lotus to a rock, waiting for it to take root."

Sokei-An began translating the *Sutra of Perfect Awakening* with his future wife, Ruth Fuller Everett. But during the Second World War his work, like that of many Japanese Americans, was interrupted by internment. His health was already poor and internment made it worse. He was released and married in 1944, but internment had severely weakened him and on May 15, 1945 he died. He charged his wife, Ruth Fuller Sasaki, with two tasks: firstly, to find a Japanese Rinzai Zen Master to replace him, and secondly, to finish the translation of the Rinzai Roku. She did a wonderful job of completing the translation during the 60s, but finding a Zen Master for the West was extremely difficult. She did, however, manage to bring Isshu Miura Roshi to New York for a while.

When Ruth Fuller Sasaki died in 1967, among her many

accomplishments was the establishment of a sub-temple of Daitokuji, to be used as a training center for Westerners to practice in Japan. This let people such as Walter Nowick complete his studies with Goto Zuigan Roshi and return to teach in Maine. Gary Snyder (the Zen poet) and Irmgaard Myokyoni Schlogel (founder of the London Zen Center) also practiced there. Schlogel brought Goto Zuigan's successor, Soko Morinaga Roshi, to England to do annual sesshin.

In the meantime, Nyogen Senzaki had moved to Los Angeles. He arrived in 1931 and stayed there until his death in 1957, except for his internment at Heart Mt., Wyoming, during World War II. Senzaki now lived as a monk. According to his own saying, "A Buddhist monk is celibate and leads the simplest life possible. He never charges for any kind of work he does, being only too grateful to do something for his fellow man. He accepts used clothes and old shoes and wears them. Any excess of food or money, he gives away. He sleeps quietly without worries, having none in his possession." Senzaki lived this teaching, encouraging the members of his "Floating Zendo" by his example.

Among his congregation was Paul Reps (Author of *Zen Flesh, Zen Bones*), who helped Senzaki to translate the *Gateless Gate* and several other books. In 1934 he started corresponding with the young Soen Nakagawa after reading some of his poems. Soen Nakagawa had a great deal of influence on western practitioners during the 60s and 70s.

After World War II, Senzaki relocated into a small bedsit at the Miyako hotel on the corner of San Pedro and First Street, in the heart of Little Tokyo. Apparently, at the time it was "filled with whores, pimps, and numbers runners." He attracted a substantial number of Practitioners for his Sunday morning services and continued to serve the American and Japanese American congregations separately. In 1948 he finally met Soen Nakagawa in San Francisco. The friendship between these two masters would create strong Dharmic connections that have an impact to this day.

In 1955 Nyogen Senzaki made his final trip to Japan. It was there that he met Tai Shimano (later Eido Roshi) at Ryotakuji. Soen Nakagawa had requested that Tai Shimano go over to America to take care of an ailing Nyogen Senzaki, but unfortunately Senzaki died before this was possible. Even so, a few years later Shimano found himself in America.

Taizan Maezumi, Sensei, (later Roshi) crossed the water from Japan to serve as a priest to the Zenshuji Soto Mission in Los Angeles. He met Nyogen Senzaki and studied with him until Senzaki's death. That year with Senzaki deeply influenced the young Maezumi, Sensei. Every New Year's day, Taizan Maezumi and the Zen Center of Los Angeles community would hold services for him at his grave and read his last words.

Friends in the Dharma, be satisfied with your own heads. Do not put on any false heads above your own. Then, minute after minute, watch your step closely. Each head of yours is the noblest thing in the whole universe. No God, No Buddha, No sage, No master can reign over it. Rinzai said, 'If you master your own situation, wherever you stand is the land of truth. How many of our fellow beings can prove the truthfulness of these words by actions?

Keep your head cool but your feet warm. Do not let sentiments sweep your feet... Remember me as a monk, nothing else. I don't belong to any sect or cathedral. None of them should send me a promoted priest's rank or anything of the sort. I like to be free from such trash and die happily.

Judge Christmas Humphreys, Founder and President of the British Buddhist Society, one of the oldest such institutions in the West.

After initially coming to America, D.T. Suzuki went back and forth to Japan, continuing his translation career. He married Beatrice Erskine in Japan in 1911. With Soyen Shaku's death in 1919, he moved to Kyoto to become a professor of "Philosophy of Religion" at Otani University. It was there that he translated essays in Zen Buddhism (first series). He traveled extensively and made quite an impression in England, meeting, among many, Alan Watts and Christmas Humphreys, the founder of the Buddhist Society (UK). Both men became influential in shaping Zen in the West: Humphreys for his constant devotion to Buddhism, especially Zen, throughout his life; and Watts for his popular works on Zen that made Zen philosophy accessible to the masses from the Beat Generation onwards. Watts, after he moved to America, married Sokei-An's stepdaughter, Eleanor Everett and did some study with Sokei-An.

With the advent of World War II, D.T. Suzuki went into seclusion, pursuing his studies. In 1949 he returned to America for an extended visit and taught a series of lectures at Columbia University. Among his students were psychoanalysts and therapists such as Erich Fromm and Karen Horney. Philip Kapleau (later Kapleau Roshi) also attended. In 1957 Suzuki was a featured speaker at the conference on Zen Buddhism and psychoanalysis in Cuernavaca, Mexico. During this conference he did much to legitimize the on-going dialogue between Zen and psychoanalysis, and had a great effect on the participants. Erich Fromm said of his presence, "A change of mood began to be apparent. Everyone became more concentrated and quiet. At the end of the meeting a visible change had occurred in many of the participants. They had gone through a unique experience: they felt that an important event had happened in their lives; that they had woken up a little; and that they would never lose what they had gained."

D.T. Suzuki achieved much in his long life with his translations, essays, and books and especially his efforts in bringing together eastern and western disciplines. His merging of Philosophy and religion brought to the forefront the questions and dialogue that were essential to bridging that gap. He died in 1966 after 70 years of going back and forth to teach.

BEAT ZEN AND THE NEW WAVE

During the 50s, the Beat Generation had a great interest in Zen. Although people like Gary Snyder did actually practice, there was more interest in Zen's philosophy. Poets like Snyder, Alan Ginsberg, Jack Kerouac, and Philip Whalen, expressed their lives in ways that held the interest of a nation. A good example of this is seen in the scripture of Golden Eternity (V.22) by Jack Kerouac.

Stare deep into the world before you as if it were/the void: Innumerable holy ghosts, bhuddies/and savior gods there hide, smiling. All the/atoms emitting light inside wavehood, there is/no personal separation of any of it. A hummingbird/ can come into a house and a hawk will not: So rest/and be assured, while looking for light. You/may suddenly be devoured by the darkness/and find the true light.

Shunryu Suzuki Roshi studied with his father's disciple Gyakuju So-On Roshi, a strict disciplinarian, and eventually succeeded him. While attending Komazawa University, he met an English woman who was an English teacher to the Crown Prince, and she ultimately became his first Western student. From this meeting he had a strong desire to practice in the West, yet after finishing his studies and training at Eiheiji his teacher would not let him. Instead, he became head priest of Zounji and, after his teacher's death, of Rinso-In, his teacher's temple. During World War II he refused to encourage the war effort through jingoistic talks, and organized discussion groups that opposed the jingoism of Japanese imperialism. After helping to rebuild Rinso-In and his country after the war, his mind returned to the vision of his youth: America.

On May 23, 1959, he flew into San Francisco on a three-year trial as priest at Sokoji Temple. After two years his family followed, in order to encourage him to return, but they stayed too. Right away he introduced za-zen, with emphasis on posture and regular practice. He would say to Americans and Japanese people, "I sit at five-thirty every morning. You are welcome to join me." Soon, many students flocked to Sokoji.

He taught the essence of Dogen's teaching: "practice and realization are one." He emphasized that, "Just sitting is the manifestation of the enlightened way. Practicing with a goal in mind is ludicrous. You miss what you are now."

This was very refreshing to those raised on D.T. Suzuki- and Kensho (enlightenment)-driven practices. This is not to say that the one is superior to the other, but that it is another face of the same reality.

Suzuki Roshi held his first seven-day sesshin in 1962. He made Zen accessible to Westerners by cutting through the mystery and putting Zen in laymen's terms. Using the term "beginner's mind", he said "In beginner's mind there is 'no thought.....I have attained something.' When we have no thought of achievement, no thought of self, we are true beginners. Everyone can do it." He would also talk about difficult Zen texts such as the *Blue Cliff Record*.

With this approach, Suzuki's popularity increased and by 1966, sixty people were sitting in the mornings. He was now assisted by Dainin Katagiri, and later by Kobun Chino, who came over from Japan. His seniors started several satellite groups: Mel Sojun Weitsman in Berkeley, Bill Kwong in Mill Valley and Marion Derby in Los Altos. By the late 60s Trudy Dixon had assembled and edited Suzuki Roshi's talks into the book *Zen Mind Beginners Mind*, one of the most popular and influential books on Zen. She died before it could be published.

In July 1966, Tassajara Zen Mountain Center was officially opened. The first formal Zen training monastery in the USA, it was a landmark for Zen in the west. Congratulations came from all over the world and without regard to sectarian lines. Suzuki Roshi's teaching could now be experienced in a traditional structure. In 1969 the San Francisco Zen Center on Page Street was opened, forming a permanent residential community in the city, and a little later, Green Gulch farm was established on the coast just north of San Francisco. By 1971 Suzuki Roshi was dying of cancer. A few weeks before he died, he installed his successor Richard Baker as abbot of San Francisco Zen Center. Richard Baker, although no longer directly affiliated to San Francisco Zen Center, is still teaching in Colorado and Germany.

After Nyogen Senzaki's death Soen Nakagawa Roshi came regularly to America. Although he was abbot of Ryutakuji, a Rinzai monastery, he had no problem donning his robes to study with Shogaku Harada Roshi, a Soto master of high renown. It is through him that he became friends with Yasutani Roshi.

In 1958 he held what is believed to have been the first formal seven-day Zen sesshin in America, as a memorial to Nyogen Senzaki. Robert Aitken was Soen's attendant.

In 1962, Soen invited Yasutani to take his place on his teaching tour of America. Robert Aitken, Philip Kapleau, Taizan Maezumi, and Tai Shimano (later Eido Roshi) assisted. In 1976, when Eido Roshi founded Dai Bosatsu Monastery in up-state New York, Soen Roshi became the first abbot.

Soen Roshi's style was somewhat eccentric. Once, he was delivering a Zen talk that involved a reference to Japanese underpants. He realized that most of his audience had no idea what they looked like, so he modestly asked the audience to turn their backs for a minute. Then he removed his underwear and asked them to turn around; holding up his underpants, he showed them what he was talking about. This childlike spontaneity, an excellent trait in a teacher, endeared him to many westerners.

There were two other influential figures at Ryutakuji at that time: Sochu Roshi, Soen's successor, who later taught in Europe and his successor Kyudo Roshi, who taught in Jerusalem and New York before assuming the duties of abbot of Ryutakuji in the early 90s. Soen Nakagawa Roshi died in 1981.

Hakuun Yasutani Roshi was ordained at the age of thirteen. He married at thirty, had a family of five, and followed a long career as a teacher, but he did not meet his true teacher until he was thirty-nine years old. His teacher Daiun Sogaku Harada Roshi was one of the few Soto masters who trained and completed Koan study in the Rinzai tradition. Following in his teacher's footsteps, Yasutani emphasized realization, something that the Soto school had failed to promote—hence much of the practice had degenerated into a loose, "just sit and everything will be O.K." attitude. Like his teacher, Yasutani Roshi felt that realization was the most important point in practice. He never failed to emphasize that point and encouraged his students to strive toward it, saying, "It is fine to say that you are enlightened, but you really have to realize it for yourself." This approach got him into trouble in the Soto school, yet he felt that he could teach the best parts of Soto and Rinzai Zen, and avoid their inexpedient aspects.

Hakuyu Taizan Maezumi
Roshi (1931–1995).

By the time Yasutani Roshi arrived in America, he was already seventy-seven years old. Between 1962 and 1969 he crisscrossed America seven times, mainly doing sesshin. His American groups included Rochester Zen Center, under Philip Kapleau; Koko-An Zendo under Robert Aitken Roshi; Dai-Bosatsu with Eido Shimano Roshi; and Zen Center of Los Angeles under Taizan Maezumi Roshi. Yasutani Roshi died on March 28, 1973, at the age of eighty-eight, three days after officiating in a precept ceremony for about thirty people. His attendant reported that Yasutani Roshi said, "I just got through that on will-power alone." He exhausted himself doing what he loved. With the death of these old masters, the teachings were handed down to a new generation.

Maezumi Roshi was a bridge between the generation of masters like Nyogen Senzaki and Suzuki Roshi and those of today. Born in 1931, he was one of eight children, five of whom became temple priests. In his childhood he had many influences; his father, Hakujun Kuroda Roshi, had built his temple from a ruin, and needed tremendous support from his congregation. He would say, "The Sangha (Buddhist community) is the most important." This phrase would stick with Taizan throughout his life. His mother, from whom he inherited the name Maezumi, selflessly served the temple, rising well before all of the monks. Seeing how his mother practiced he realized that women had a lot to contribute to practice, and vowed to honor their role.

During Taizan's formative years Joko Roshi would sometimes hold sesshin at the Kuroda's temple. When he was sixteen he was sent by Kuroda Roshi to stay at the Hannya Dojo in Tokyo, while he was studying at college. The resident teacher was Koryu Osaka Roshi, the main successor of Joko Roshi and a lay teacher. Maezumi started Koan study with Koryu Roshi but because he left for America he would not finish his study for another 20 years. Later he went to study at Sojiji Temple, and in 1955 had Dharma Transmission from his father Kuroda Roshi.

In 1956 he set sail for Los Angeles with $300 and a suitcase. Arriving at Zenshuji temple, he assisted the abbot Reirin Yamada Roshi, with whom he studied Dogen's Shobogenzo. He began learning English and supported himself with all kinds of jobs, including fortune cookie writer and houseboy. By 1967 he felt it was time to set up independently, so he bought a house on Serrano street in Los Angeles and a year later the Zen Center of Los Angeles moved to its present location on Normandie Avenue. In the early days he had much support from two of his brothers, Takeshi Kuroda Roshi, and Junyu Koroda Roshi. Takeshi Kuroda started a non-profitmaking organization, the Zenkoji Scholarship Fund, which helps foster the understanding of Buddhism. This scholarship exchange has done much to promote the mutual understanding of practitioners, from West and East.

Meanwhile Yasutani Roshi and Koryu Roshi visited ZCLA regularly to hold sesshin, and Taizan Maezumi returned to Japan for several extended visits to complete koan study. Yasutani Roshi gave Maezumi Roshi the Inka (certificate of a fully independent teacher) in 1970. A year later Koryu Roshi also gave him Inka. By 1976 Bernie Glassman, whose work was essential in establishing ZCLA, was ready for Dharma Transmission and in 1979 he moved to New York to open his Greyston center.

By 1981 ZCLA owned most of a city block, with 120 residents, and a country property, later called Yokoji Zen Mountain Center.

A few years later, four of Maezumi Roshi's successors were ready to become independent: Dennis Genpo Merzel, now based in Utah and doing a lot of work in Europe, Charlotte Joko Beck in San Diego, Jan Chozen Bays in Portland, and Jerry Shishin Wick in Colorado.

Maezumi Roshi had many difficulties and yet he persevered through it all, building the community and deepening the practice. He frequently quoted his favorite Mexican phrase, *poco a poco*, little by little.

By the time of his death in 1995, he had produced 12 successors. Besides those previously mentioned are John Daido Loori, of Zen Mountain Monastery in upstate New York; John Tesshin Sanderson, Mexico City; Fred Jitsudo Ancheta, Albuquerque, New Mexico; Charles Tenshin Fletcher, Yokoji Zen Mountain Center, in Mountain Center California; Susan Myoyu Palmer, Des Plains, Illinois; Nicolee Jikyo Miller-McMahon, San Diego; and William Nyogen Yeo, Los Angeles.

Two weeks before he died Maezumi Roshi gave Inka to Bernie Tetsugen Glassman, his first Dharma heir. Throughout his career in America, he had worked for a strong independent American Soto Zen Buddhist organization with friendly ties to Japan. Just before his death in 1995, he felt this was accomplished with the start of the Soto Zen Buddhists of America (SZBA). Although this organization is only partially active as yet, it promises to foster unity among the diverse American Soto Zen groups, and be a registry for American Practitioners, so that they do not have to rely on Japan.

> Please take good care of yourself. This is always the best way to take care of everything. In your daily life, please accept yourself as you are and your life as it is. Be intimate with yourself. I want you to take good advantage of every chance you have to be a truly intimate being.

Maezumi Roshi (1931–1995)

Joshu Sasaki Roshi came to Los Angeles in 1962. A master of the Yoshenji line of Rinzai Zen, he first taught out of a garage in Gardenia before moving to a large mission-style compound, the Cimerron Zen Center (now called Rinzai-ji) in Los Angeles. Later he started the Mountain Training Center at Mount Baldy and Bodhi Mandala in New Mexico. Since then, affiliates have sprung up in North Carolina, Alberqueque, Phoenix, Vancouver, Puerto Rico, and Vienna. His style is traditional Rinzai, with koans used in a non-traditional fashion tailored to the West. He has yet to name a successor, but has many senior students.

Phillip Kapleau returned to America in 1965 after spending thirteen years in Japan, studying first with Soen Roshi and then with Yasutani Roshi. Just before he returned, he published *The Three Pillars of Zen*, a book that is still regarded as an excellent introduction to Zen practice. He continued to study with Yasutani Roshi until 1967, when major disagreements concerning the Americanization of Zen arose between them, especially concerning the chanting of the Heart Sutra in English. This ultimately destroyed their relationship. Kapleau Roshi established a strong practice community around Rochester, New York and that legacy flourishes today. Kapleau Roshi has several successors and many affiliate groups around the country.

Robert Aitken Roshi happened to be working in Guam as a construction worker when hostilities with Japan broke out in 1941. He was captured, then interned near Kobe, Japan, where a guard loaned him a book called *Zen and The Art of English Literature* by R.H. Blyth. Blyth was a disciple of D.T. Suzuki, and in 1944, Aitken and Blyth finally met while they were still interned. A firm friendship was established between them. This meeting with Blyth sparked Aitken's interest in Zen and encouraged him to seek out a true Zen Master. After returning to the States and finishing his BA in English Literature, he heard about Nyogen Senzaki, who put him in contact with Soen Roshi at Ryutakiji. Soen Roshi in turn put him in touch with Yasutani Roshi, and Aitken settled down to study with him. He studied with Yasutani Roshi for many years and eventually finished his training with Koun Yamada Roshi, Yasutani Roshi's main successor.

Za-zen meditation at Zen Center Los Angeles (early 1980s).

In 1959, Robert Aitken and his wife Anne established a lay practice center, the Diamond Sangha at the Koko An Zendo, in Maui, Hawaii. This eventually grew into two other centers in Honolulu, Hawaii. Robert Aitken continued Yamada Roshi's lay line, encouraging vital lay practice and engagement in everyday activities. One aspect of his interest in social engagement can be seen in his role in the Buddhist Peace Fellowship, a group of socially conscious Buddhist activists. From the late '60s on, he continued to develop the two centers on Hawaii, eventually spreading his teachings onto the US mainland and establishing many affiliate centers, especially in California. He also has groups in Australia and Europe. Before he retired from active teaching in 1996, he had several successors, including Nelson Foster, who is currently head of the Diamond Sangha, John Tarrent, a Jungian Psychotherapist and Pat Hawk, a Catholic Priest. Aitken Roshi is the author of several books and his lay lineage has had a marked influence on Zen practice today.

Tai Shimano (Eido Roshi), as you may remember, had been asked by Soen Roshi to take care of Nyogen Senzaki in Los Angeles. Unfortunately, Senzaki died before Shimano could leave Japan. However, Soen Roshi decided to send Shimano to Hawaii to assist the fledgling Koko-an Zendo as resident monk. By 1964 he was ready for a change, feeling that Hawaii was more of a place for vacation than Zen practice. He arrived in New York with a suitcase and a *kyosaku* (awakening stick) and proceeded to set up a zendo in his home. One by one, people began to participate.

The Zen Studies Society, a society founded by Cornelius Crane that was set up to spread the works of D.T. Suzuki and to "introduce the cultural, educational, and spiritual aspects of Zen Buddhism to the West", was inactive at that time, so Tai Shimano negotiated to adopt and re-activate it as his own organization. This move proved to be very successful and by 1968 he was able to formally open the New York Shoboji temple (Temple of the True Dharma).

During these formative years, he persevered with his studies with both Soen and Yasutani Roshi and assisted them with their American tours. By 1972 Soen Roshi had certified Tai Shimano, now Eido Roshi, to teach. At this point Eido Roshi started to develop his plans for a mountain monastery, and by 1976 his plans reached fruition and Dai Bosatsu monastery was formally opened. Dai Bosatsu is one of the few examples of traditional Japanese temple design and construction. Eido Roshi has taught his style of Traditional Rinzai Zen practice from the founding of Dai Bosatsu up to the present day.

The first Western woman to complete Soto Zen training in Japan was Jiyu Kennett. Born in England in 1924, she started practicing with the London Buddhist Vihara from an early age. By the late 1950s she was lecturing at the London Buddhist Society, yet she yearned for more intensive practice. This yearning led her to Malaysia, where she was ordained in a Rinzai monastery as a monk. Still not satisfied, she finally ended up in Japan in 1962 at Sojiji Temple (one of the two main temples of the Soto Sect). It was a very difficult time for westerners, especially for women. To make things worse, her teacher Keido Chisan felt that westerners couldn't practice Zen. Yet she persevered and was accepted into the monastery, and was able to live in a small sub-temple. She eventually reached the position of Guest-master, a high position for a westerner.

Jiyu Kennett received transmission before her teacher died in 1968. She studied for another year in Japan and then left for her homeland. The religious climate in England in 1969 seemed closed to her teachings, so she headed out west to America, where she was greeted with open arms. By 1970 Shasta Abbey was open in northern California as a Soto Zen training monastery, and from there she began to establish many affiliate centers throughout America and England. Throssel Hole Priory in Northumbria remains as the only Zen training monastery in England today.

Right from the start Kennett Roshi worked on westernizing the Zen form and liturgy. Her style has a unique Episcopalian flavor, yet the essential core of Zen training is apparent. Her translations of Japanese Zen ceremonies have proved invaluable, and in some cases are still the only ones available.

The years of practice in Japan seriously affected Kennett Roshi's health, yet despite this difficulty she taught constantly for almost thirty years. Finally her health gave out and she died in 1996, leaving Rev. Eko Little in charge of Shasta Abbey.

Dainin Katagiri Roshi had been invited over from Japan to assist Shunryu Suzuki Roshi in the 1960s. After Suzuki Roshi's death in 1971, he helped during the transition period, then in 1972 he founded the Minnesota Zen Meditation Center, (Ganshoji). The influences on his teaching style came from his training at Eiheiji monastery and especially from his own teacher Kaigai Docho, who had the reputation of being a tough, disciplined teacher. Although Katagiri Roshi embodied that traditional style, he exuded a personal warmth and elegance that shone through his tough exterior. Eventually he established several practice centers in the Mid-West, including Hokyoji (his mountain monastery) and the Nebraska Zen Center. Before his passing away in 1990, he left twelve successors, eight of whom are actively teaching today. His traditional teachings, combined with an open Western style, are maintained through successors such as Nonin Chowaney running the Nebraska Zen Center; Shoken Winecoff, the Kearney Zendo; and Karen Sekijun Sunna, the Minnesota Zen Meditation Center.

THE BRIDGE TO THE 21ST CENTURY

Shunryu Suzuki Roshi left one successor, Richard Baker Roshi; however, there were other students of Suzuki Roshi who did much to further Zen in America.

Both Bill Jakusho Kwong and Mel Sojun Weitsman received transmission from Suzuki Roshi's son Hoitsu. Kwong Roshi established his center at Sonoma mountain, Northern California, and from this base he travels to Poland to teach. Mel Sojun Weitsman opened the Berkeley Zen Center in 1967 and has kept his close ties with San Francisco Zen Center. During the difficult times of the mid-80s he was invited to become co-abbot with Reb Tenshin Anderson Roshi, a successor of Baker Roshi, and assist in the running of the center. Both Weitsman Roshi and Anderson Roshi have retired as abbots of San Francisco Zen Center; Anderson Roshi is currently the resident teacher at Green Gulch and Weitsman Roshi continues at Berkeley. Both have several successors, two of whom, Blanche Hartman and Norman Fischer, are at present co-abbots of the San Francisco Zen Center.

The members of Suzuki Roshi's lineage have extensive experience with Buddhist community life and form the oldest and most solid group in the West. They have produced beautiful translations of Zen and Buddhist writings that have given renewed appreciation to practice.

In the 70s and 80s many second-generation teachers began their independent teaching careers. Roshis Richard Baker, Mel Weitsman, Bill Kwong and Reb Anderson have been mentioned. In Maezumi Roshi's lineage Bernie Glassman Roshi started the Greyston Center in Riverdale, New York. He then moved to a poor district of Yonkers, where he could practice Zen as social action. He opened a bakery employing Zen students and locals. Over a period of 15 years of exhaustive effort, he also opened housing projects for local families with built-in childcare and an Aids clinic. At the same time, he and his community were developing inter-faith programs and translation work. His successors embody Glassman Roshi's diversity: Peter Muryo Mathieson, a renowned writer; Father Jinsen Kennedy Roshi, a Jesuit Priest; Don Singer Sensei, a Rabbi; Wendy Egyoku Nakao and Anne Seisen Fletcher, leaders of Centers founded by Maezumi Roshi. In 1997 he co-founded the international Zen Peacemaker Order with his successor Sandra Jishu Holmes, Sensei. The Order is deeply rooted in the practice of meditation, engaged spirituality, and interfaith expression.

Genpo Merzel Roshi left ZCLA in 1984 to establish a "floating Zendo," the Kanzeon Sangha, traveling over Europe and the United States. He along with Deshimaru Roshi, Soen-sa nim and Kapleau Roshi were among the first Zen teachers to do regular sesshin and establish centers in Europe. Although there are many practicing Zen Buddhists in Europe, there are very few fully certified Zen training centers. Earlier pioneers such as Deshimaru Roshi who established his training center in France did much, yet after Deshimaru Roshi's death much of the Zen teaching was performed by non-resident teachers such as Genpo Roshi. Finally in 1994 he settled down in Salt Lake City, the base for the Kanzeon Sangha and the local training center hosting practitioners from all over the world. Two of his successors are Europeans: Catherine Genno Pages teaches in Paris, France, and Anton Tenkei Coppens, is based in Holland.

One of the most successful training monasteries at the present time is Zen Mountain Monastery, developed by John Daido Loori Roshi. Daido Roshi left ZCLA with Glassman Roshi in 1980 to help develop the Zen Center of New York. In 1980 Daido Roshi purchased an old monastery in the Catskills and struggled to keep it afloat. The first few years were difficult; however, now it has many affiliates around the States and New Zealand. Because of Daido Roshi's skill in art and publishing, the Zen Mountain Monastery has become adept at promoting Zen through various modern media, including publications, video, and computer. Yet the primary focus is the diligent practice of za-zen.

INFLUENCES

Today in America there has been a shift. Zen teachers are no longer a rare commodity; rather, they are spreading all over the country and fulfilling local needs.

Diversity is also a mark of American Zen; not only are there differing lines of both Soto and Rinzai, but there is also a great deal of influence from Korean Zen, especially through Soen-Sa-Nim and his successors in the Kwan-Um school, who have centers all over the world. Tich Nhat Hahn—with his brand of Vietnamese Zen emphasizing the practice of peace and mindfulness—has popularized and affected many who already practice Zen.

Tibetan and Theravadin Buddhism have affected many Zen students through the plethora of books available on the subjects and their retreats and seminars. Buddhism does not just have a Japanese face; it changes to address the needs of the people.

The dialogue between Zen and psychotherapy has been ongoing since the 50s and now several Zen teachers are also psychotherapists, including John Tarrant Roshi and Jikyo Miller-McMahon, Sensei. Nowadays, people have a lot more access to these methods of addressing deep-seated habitual patterns that could hinder practitioners for decades.

Contact between Zen and Christian practitioners has taken place since the first Catholic missionaries landed in Japan with the Portuguese in the 16th century. After World War II, heightened interest in Eastern religion and philosophy brought several Jesuit priests to study with Japanese Zen masters. Others, such as Thomas Merton, succeeded in re-establishing meditative practices into the Christian Religion while at the same time promoting an interest in Zen. By the 1980s, Catholic priests were returning from Japan as certified teachers of Zen. Fathers LaSalle and Yaeger are examples of this trend, with Father LaSalle teaching in Switzerland and Father Yaeger in Germany. The

Genpo Merzel Roshi, Abbot Kanzeon Sangha.

Sanbo Kyodan lineage, through Roshis Yasutani, Yamada, and Aitken, has been instrumental in that trend. Glassman Roshi, with his broad net of inter-faith practice, has certified Father Jinsen Kennedy and Rabbi Don Singer. A Sufi practitioner, Lex Hixon, died just prior to his succession.

That is one direction of interest, yet it must be remembered that most Westerners have been raised Christian or Jewish. Therefore that religious upbringing is at the back of our minds, and is bound to affect the way we practice Zen. As Zen has aided in re-establishing the meditative/contemplative aspect of the Judeo-Christian religions, conversely these religions have stimulated interest in social action. In seems that religion is not much of a barrier among those who practice, and the interface between these approaches to the truth is definitely vitalizing practice on all sides of the fence.

There are marked differences between oriental and occidental cultures and values. One obvious difference between these two cultures is in how the individual is regarded. In the West there is an appreciation of strong individuality, whereas in the East there is more pressure for the individual to conform. In the forge of practice in the midst of these forces, a new approach is being formed.

Customs, rituals, and social structures are different, and the structure and function of Zen training centers in the west reflects those differences. Experiments with the forms used in Zen Practice are occurring in most Zen centers. Some practitioners, including Toni Packer, a successor of Kapleau Roshi, and Joko Beck, a successor of Maezumi Roshi, have reduced the form to its simplest; others have only slightly modified it, while Roshis like Jiyu Kennett have created a Christian ambiance.

One thing is for sure: practice is equally open to all. Women in the West have jumped right in and have taken this truth to be their birthright. Equal opportunity is a fact in the majority of Zen Centers, and if position or recognition is deserved, it is rewarded regardless not only of gender, but also of race and sexual orientation. Women have taken on all kinds of roles, from teacher through to all aspects of Zen Center functions.

In summary, the most visible aspect of Western training is that men and women practice together in the West and practice separately in the East. Zen is not fixed to a particular form or approach, and just like the periods of cultural adaptation in China and Japan, Zen will conform to the cultural and spiritual needs of its host country. Yet the essential truth remains the same!

GLOSSARY OF GENERAL AND MONASTIC ZEN TERMS

Aanuttara-samyak-sambodhi: All penetrating, perfect enlightenment.

Amitabha: The mythical Buddha of the Western Paradise much revered in the Judo Shien Shu sect of Japanese Buddhism on the basis that by his saving grace realization can be attained.

Ango: Three months' intensive training period.

Arhat: One who is worthy and free from craving. This is the ideal of the Hinayana or Southern School of Buddhism.

Avalokiteshvara: The principal Bodhisattva in the Zen Buddhist tradition. Avalokiteshvara embodies boundless compassion for all sentient beings and is represented in male and female form. In Japan best known in female form, this Bodhisattva is called Kannon or Kanzen.

Blue Cliff Record (Jap. **Hekiganroku**): A collection of one hundred koan compiled, with appreciatory verse, by Master Hsueh-tou Ch'ung-hsien (Jap. Setcho Juken, 980–1052) and with commentaries by Master Yuan-wu k'o-Ch'in (Jap. Ebgo Kokugon, 1063–1135).

Bodhi: Sanskrit for enlightenment. Bodhi mind is an awakened mind.

Bodhisattva: One who practices the Buddha way, but who out of compassion for other sentient beings puts off his own enlightenment to help all to be free and awakened. This is the ideal of Mahayana, a Northern

School of Buddhism of which Zen is a part.

Buddha: Enlightened one. Shakyamuni Buddha refers to the historical Buddha, literally sage of the Shakya clan.

Buddha Way: The path to enlightenment taught by the Buddha.

Butsu: Japanese for Buddha.

Ch'an: Chinese word for the Sanskrit word *Dhyana* (meaning meditation). Name given to Chinese school of Buddhism founded by Bodhidharma. Translated into Japanese becomes Zen.

Daisan: Interviews with Zen instructor.

Dennan: Altar attendant; distributes sutra books.

Densho: Large hanging bell that announces services.

Dharma: Sanskrit word meaning "The Law." Used in a variety of ways. May mean the teachings of the Buddha, the whole body of Buddhist literature, universal truth, self nature, or just "the way."

Dhyana: See **Ch'an**.

Diamond Sutra: A portion of the *Prajna Paramita Sutra* much valued in the Zen tradition.

Doan: Person who hits bell and gongs during service.

Dogen: A great figure in the history of Zen. Born in Japan in 1200, Dogen founded the Japanese Soto school of Zen. He is the author of *Shobogenzo*, which means *The Eye of The True Law*, an important collection of Dharma essays.

Dokusan: Interviews with a Roshi.

Dukkha: The First Noble Truth taught by the Buddha. Translated as "suffering," dukkha is said to originate from desire (see **Four Noble Truths**). Dukkha may also be understood as the underlying unsatisfactory nature of life experienced by most people.

Eight-fold Path: The path leads to liberation, consisting of right understanding, right aim, right speech, right action, right livelihood, right effort, right mindfulness, and right concentration.

Enlightenment (also **Satori**): The direct experience and realization of one's true nature (also called one's Buddha nature).

Four Noble Truths: Fundamental teaching of the Buddha concerning human life. They are:
1. life is suffering (dukkha);
2. suffering has a cause;
3. there is a way to put an end to the cause of suffering;
4. the way to put an end to the cause of suffering is the Eight-fold Path.

Fusatsu: Renewal of vows ceremony.

Fushinzamu: Community work.

Gaitan: Front and back porches.

Gateless Gate: A collection of forty-eight koans compiled, with commentary and appreciatory verse, by Wu-men Hu-k'ai (Jap. Mumon Ekai) in the 13th century.

Han: Hanging wooden block, struck to announce za-zen period.

Heart Sutra: A condensed version of the *Prajna Paramita Sutra* highlighting the most important teachings.

Hosan: Days off.

Ino: Head leader of chanting.

Jikido: Timekeeper during za-zen.

Jiko: Officiant of services attendant, carries the incense box.

Jisha: Officiant or teacher's attendant.

Jukai: Buddhist ceremony in which the Zen student makes a commitment to maintain the precepts.

Junko: Walking with the Awakening stick.

Kensho: Literally means seeing into one's nature; it is the experience of satori.

Kinhin: Walking meditation.

Koan: Originally, it meant a public case which established a legal precedent. In Zen it is an apparently paradoxical story assigned to a student to solve, in order to help their awakening or to test the deepness of their realization. There are about 1700 recorded koans (pronounced in Japanese ko-an). Notable collections may be found in the *Mumonkan* (*The Gateless Gate*) and the *Hekiganroku* (*The Blue Cliff Record*).

Kyosaku: Awakening stick.

Mokugyo: Wooden fish—wood drum that keeps beat during services.

Mu: As used in the koan "Joshua's Dog": Chao-chou (778–897) was asked by a monk, "Does a dog have Buddha nature?" He replied, "Mu!" It is a meaningless exclamation pointing directly at Reality. Often the first koan given to a Zen student.

Nenju: Literally, the ten Buddha names. A thanksgiving ceremony performed in a Zen monastery at the end of a formal week of practice and before a day off.

Oryoki: Formal meals, eating out of three bowls.

Paramitas: The six perfections practiced by Bodhisattvas. The Paramitas include wisdom (*prajna*), patience (*kshanti*), generosity (*dana*), meditative awareness (*Dhyana*), effort (*virya*), and precepts (*sila*).

Prajna: Wisdom in which discriminating consciousness and all dualism have been transcended.

Precepts: The sixteen precepts are: the Three Treasures (be one with the Buddha, be one with the Dharma, be one with the Sangha); the Three Pure Precepts (do not commit evil, do good, do good for others); the Ten Grave Precepts (do not kill, do not steal, do not be greedy, do not lie, do not be ignorant, do not talk about others' faults, do not elevate yourself by criticizing others, do not be stingy, do not get angry, do not speak ill of the Three Treasures).

Roshi: Head teacher, Zen Master.

Samadhi: One-pointed, non-dualistic awareness.

Samu: Work.

Sangha: Buddhist priesthood or monastic order or simply a community of Buddhists. Also implies the harmonious relationship of all sentient beings.

Satori: Enlightenment. The experience of realizing one's true nature.

Sensei: Certified teacher.

Sesshin: A Zen retreat, a period of intensive Zen practice. Usually seven days long.

Shikantaza: Just to sit. Za-zen without the exercises or breath counting or koan study.

Shuso: Head training monk for three-month period.

Shuso Hossen: Ceremony of testing Shuso's understanding.

Sutra: Buddhist scriptures or texts recording works attributed directly to the Buddha or to other enlightened Buddhist teachers.

Tan: Woven rice straw mats.

Tenzo: Head cook.

Za-zen: Seated meditation. In Zen, za-zen is also used to describe generally the exercises of breath counting, shikantaza, and koan study, practiced while in the za-zen position.

Zabutan: Square sitting mats.

Zafu: Round sitting cushions.

Zendo: Main meditation hall.

FURTHER READING

Aitken, R., *Taking the Path of Zen* (North Point Press, 1982).

App, U., trans., *Master Yunmen* (Kodansha, 1994).

Bancroft, A., *Zen, Direct Pointing at Reality* (London: Thames & Hudson, 1979).

Bielefeldt, C., *Dogen's Manuals of Zen Meditation* (University of California Press, 1988).

Blofeld, J., *The Wheel of Life* (London: Rider, 1959).

Blofeld, J., *The Zen Teaching of Huang Po* (The Buddhist Society, 1968–1985).

Blomberg, C., *The Heart of the Warrior* (Kent: Japan Library, 1994).

Blyth, R.H., *Zen and the Zen Classics* (Tokyo: Hokuseido Press, 1962).

Braverman, A., *Warrior of Zen* (New York: Kodansha International, 1994).

Carrithers, M., *The Buddha* (Oxford University Press, 1983).

Castile, R., *The Way of Tea* (Tokyo: Weatherhill, 1971).

Claremon, N., *Zen in Motion* (Vermont: Inner Traditions International Ltd, 1991).

Claxton, G., (Ed.), *Beyond Therapy* (Wisdom, 1986).

Claxton, G., *The Heart of Buddhism* (Crucible, 1990).

Cleary, C., trans., *The Book of Serenity* (Lindisfarne Press, 1990).

Cleary, C., trans., *Swampland Flowers: The Letters and Lectures of Zen Master Ta Hui* (New York: Grove Press, 1977).

Cleary, T. and Cleary, J.C., trans., *The Blue Cliff Record* (3 vols.) (Boulder: Shambhala, 1977).

Cleary, T., *The Book of Five Rings* (Boston & London: Shambhala, 1993).

Cleary, T., *The Inner Teachings of Taoism* (Boston & London: Shambhala).

Cleary, T., *The Japanese Art of War* (Boston & London: Shambhala, 1991).

Collcutt, *Five Mountains: The Rinzai Zen Monastic Institution in Medieval Japan* (Cambridge, Mass.: Harvard U.P., 1981).

Cook, H., *Samurai: The Story of a Warrior Tradition* (London: Blandford Press, 1993).

Cook, *Transmission of the Light* (Center Publications, 1991).

Crook, J., *Catching a Feather on a Fan* (London: Harper Collins, 1991).

Crook, J. and Fontana, D. (Eds), *Space in Mind* (Dorset: Element Books, 1990).

De Mente, Boye, *The Whole Japan Book* (Phoenix Books, 1983).

Deshimaru, T., *The Ring of the Way* (London: Rider, 1988).

Deshimaru, T., *The Zen Way to the Martial Arts* (London: Rider, 1983).

Dogen and Uchiyama, trans. Thomas Wright, *Refining Your Life* (New York and Tokyo: Weatherhill, 1983).

Dogen Zenji, trans. Cleary, T., *Shobogenzo: Zen Essays by Dogen Zenji* (Honolulu: University of Hawaii Press, 1986).

Dumoulin, H., *A History of Zen Buddhism* (New York: Random House, 1963. London: Faber & Faber, 1968).

Dumoulin, H., *Zen Enlightenment* (Tokyo: Weatherhill, 1979).

Durckheim, K. G. Von, *Hara The Vital Centre of Man* (London: Mandala Books, 1977).

Durckheim, K. G. Von, *Our Twofold Origin* (London: George Allan & Unwin, 1983).

Durckheim, K. G. Von, *The Japanese Cult of Tranquility* (London: Rider, 1974).

Eppstein, F. (Ed.), *The Path of Compassion* (Parallax Press, 1988).

Fields, *How the Swans Came to the Lake* (Boston & London: Shambhala, 1992).

Foulk, 'Daily Life in the Assembly', *Ten Directions* (Zen Center of Los Angeles, Spring/Summer 1991).

Friday, K. F. with Humitake, S., *Legacies of the Sword* (Honolulu: University of Hawai'i Press, 1997).

Fromm, E. and Suzuki, D.T., *Zen Buddhism and Psychoanalysis* (Souvenir Press, 1974).

Fung Yu Lan, *The Spirit of Chinese Philosophy* (London: Routledge & Kegan Paul, 1962).

Glassman, B. and Fields, R., *Instructions To The Cook* (London: Random House, 1997).

Goddard, *A Buddhist Bible* (Beacon Press, 1970).

Hakuin, trans. Yampolsky, P., *Selected Writings* (New York: Columbia University Press, 1971).

Hamada, H. T., *Spirit of Japanese Classical Martial Arts: Historical and Philosophical Perspectives* (Iowa: Kendall/Hunt Publishing Co., 1990).

Harding, D., *On Having No Head* (London: Routledge & Kegan Paul, 1986).

Harrison, E. J. and Fisher, T., *The Fighting Spirit of Japan* (London: Unwin, 1913).

Haskel, P., trans., *Bankei Zen* (New York: Grove Press, 1984).

Hayashiya, T., Nakamura, M. and Hayashiya, S., *Japanese Arts and the Tea Ceremony* (Tokyo: Weatherhill, 1974).

Herrigel, E., *Zen in the Art of Archery* (London: Routledge & Kegan Paul, 1968).

Hirai, K., *Feudal Architecture of Japan* (Tokyo: Weatherhill, 1973).

Hirose, N., *Immovable Wisdom* (Dorset: Element Books Ltd, 1992).

Hui Hai, trans. Blofeld, J., *The Zen Teaching of Instantaneous Awakening* (Leicester: Buddhist Publishing Group, 1987).

Humphries, C., *Sixty years of Buddhism in England* (London: The Buddhist Society, 1968).

Humphries, C., *Zen Buddhism* (London: Heinemann, 1949).

Ito, T., *The Japanese Garden: An Approach to Nature* (New Haven: Yale U.P., 1972).

Kammer, R., trans. Fitzgerald, B. J., *Zen and Confucius in the Art of Swordsmanship* (London: Routledge & Kegan Paul, 1978).

Kapleau, P., *The Buddhist Case For Vegetarianism* (London: Rider, 1982).

Kapleau, P., *Zen Merging of East and West* (Anchor Books, 1980).

Katz, N. (Ed.), *Buddhist and Western Psychology* (Boston & London: Shambhala, 1983).

King, W. L., *Zen and the Way of the Sword* (New York: Oxford University Press Inc., 1993).

Kiyota, M., *Kendo Its Philosophy, History and Means to Personal Growth* (London and New York: Kegan Paul International, 1995). Kobayashi, K., *Shojin Cookery* (San Francisco: The Buddhist Bookstore, 1977).

Kraft, *Eloquent Zen* (Hawaii Press, 1992).

Kraft, K. (Ed.), *Zen Traditions and Transition* (London: Rider, 1988).

Kushner, K., *One Arrow One Life* (London: Arkana, 1988).

Leggett, T., *The Dragon Mask* (London: Ippon Books, 1997).

Leggett, T., *Encounters in Yoga and Zen* (London: Routledge & Kegan Paul, 1982).

Leggett, T., *Finger and Moons* (Leicester: Buddhist Publishing Group, 1988).

Leggett, T., *A First Zen Reader* (Tokyo: Tuttle, 1960).

Leggett, T., *A Second Zen Reader* (Tokyo: Charles E. Tuttle Company, 1988).

Leggett, T., *Three Ages of Zen* (Tokyo: Charles E. Tuttle, 1993).

Leggett, T., *The Warrior Koans* (London: Arkana, 1985).

Leggett, T., *Zen and the Ways* (London: Routledge & Kegan Paul, 1978).

Linssen, R., *Zen, The Art of Life* (Pyramid, 1969).

Liu I-Ming, trans. Cleary, T., *Awakening To The Tao* (Boston & London: Shambhala, 1989).

Loori, J.D., *Mountain Record of Zen Talks* (Boston & London: Shambhala, 1988).

Low, A., *An Invitation to Practice Zen* (Tokyo: Charles E. Tuttle, 1989).

Luk, C. *Chan and Zen Teaching Vols.1-3* (Boston & London: Shambhala, 1987).

Maliszewski, M., *Spiritual Dimensions of the Martial Arts* (Tokyo: Charles E. Tuttle, 1996).

Merzel, D.G., *The Eye Never Sleeps (Striking to the Heart of Zen)* (Boston & London: Shambhala, 1991).

Merzel, D.G., *Beyond Sanity and Madness* (Tokyo: Charles E. Tuttle, 1994).

Mitchell, *The Buddha, His Life Retold* (Paragon House, 1991).

Morikawa, J. S., *The Secret of the Target* (New York: Routledge & Kegan Paul, 1988).

Neng, H., trans. Yampolsky, P., *The Platform Sutra of the 6th Patriarch* (New York: Columbia University Press, 1967).

Newman, J., *Bushido The Way of the Warrior* (Leicester: Magna Books, 1989).

Noma, S., *The Arts of Japan*, vol. 1 (Tokyo and New York: Kodansha International, 1967).

Nukariya, K., *The Religion of the Samurai* (London: Luzac & Co. Ltd, 1913, reprinted 1973).

Okakura, K., *The Book of Tea* (New York: Dover, 1964).

Okumura, S., and Leighton, T. D., trans., *The Wholehearted Way* (Tuttle, 1994).

Price, A.F., and Mou-Lan, W., (trans.), *The Diamond Sutra and The Sutra of Hui* Neng (Boston & London: Shambhala, 1969).

Rahula, W., *What the Buddha Taught* (Gordon Fraser, 1972).

Roshi, K.U., *Approach to Zen* (Japan Publications Inc., 1973).

Sadler, A. L. and Sadler. M., *Cha-no-Yu*, Kobe and London: Tuttle, 1993).

Sansom, G., *A History of Japan to 1334* (Dawson and Sons Ltd, 1978).

Sato, H., *The Sword And the Mind* (New York: The Overlook Press, 1994).

Schloegl, I. trans., *The Record of Rinzai* (London: The Buddhist Society, 1975).

Schloegl, I., *The Zen Way* (Sheldon Press, 1977).

Scott, D., and Doubleday, T., *The Elements of Zen* (Dorset: Element Books, 1992).

Sekida, K. trans., *Two Zen Classics: Mumonkan & Hekiganroku* (New York & Tokyo: Weatherhill, 1977).

Sekida, K., *Zen Training* (New York & Tokyo: Weatherhill, 1975). *Shambala Dictionary of Buddhism and Zen* (Boston & London: Shambhala, 1991).

Shimizu, Y. and Wheelwright, C., *Japanese Ink Paintings* (Princeton: Princeton U.P., 1976).

Shin'ichi, H., *Zen and the Fine Arts* (Tokyo and New York: Kodansha International, 1971).

Smart, N., *The Long Search* (London: BBC, 1977).

Sogen, O., *An Introduction to Zen Training* (London & New York: Kegan Paul International, 1996).

Sollier, A. and Gyorbiro, Z., *Japanese Archery Zen in Action* (Tokyo: Weatherhill, 1969).

Stein, H. J., *Kyudo The Art of Zen Archery* (Dorset: Element, 1988).

Stevens, J., *The Sword of No-Sword* (Boston & London: Shambhala, 1984)

Storry, R., *The Way of the Samurai* (London: Orbis Publishing, 1978).

Sugawara, M., *Lives of Master Swordsmen* (Tokyo: The East Publications Inc., 1988).

Sunim, M. S., *Heart Sutra* (Primary Point Press, 1991).

Suzuki, D.T., *An Introduction to Zen Buddhism* (London: Rider, 1969).

Suzuki, D.T., *Manual of Zen Buddhism* (London: Rider, 1950).

Suzuki, D.T., *Zen and Japanese Culture* (New Jersey: Princeton University Press, 1970).

Suzuki, S., *Zen Mind Beginners' Mind* (New York & Tokyo: Weatherhill, 1970).

Takagi, T., trans. Matsuno, T., *A Comparison of Bushi-do & Chivalry* (1914, republished Osaka: T M International Academy, 1984).

Thomas, E.J., *The Life of the Buddha* (Kegan Paul, 1949).

Trungpa, C., *Cutting Through Spiritual Materialism* (Boulder: Shambhala, 1973).

Trungpa, C., *The Myth of Freedom* (Boulder: Shambhala, 1976).

Turnbull, S. R., *The Samurai A Military History* (New York: Macmillan, 1977).

Warner, G. and Draeger, D. F., *Japanese Swordsmanship* (New York & Tokyo: Weatherhill, 1982).

Watts, A.W., *The Way of Zen* (Thames & Hudson, 1960).

Welwood J. (Ed.), *The Awakening of the Heart* (Boston & London: Shambhala, 1983).

Wilber, K., *No Boundary (Eastern and Western Approaches to Personal Growth)* (Boston & London: Shambhala, 1981).

Wilber, K., *Up From Eden* (Routledge & Kegan Paul, 1983).

Wilson, W. Scott, trans., *Ideals of the Samurai* (California: Ohara Publications, 1982).

Wilson, W. Scott, *The Unfettered Mind* (Tokyo: Kodansha, 1986).

Wright, *Buddhism in Chinese History* (Stanford University Press, 1979).

Wu, John C. H., *The Golden Age of Zen* (Image Books, 1996).

Yamada, *The Gateless Gate* (Arizona Press, 1990).

Yoneda, S., *Good Food From a Japanese Temple* (Tokyo: Kodansha, 1982).

INDEX